THAI-ENGLISH
ENGLISH-THAI
DICTIONARY AND PHRASEBOOK

D0052364

THAI-ENGLISH
ENGLISH-THAI
DICTIONARY AND PHRASEBOOK

James Higbie

HIPPOCRENE BOOKS, INC.
New York

THE AUTHOR: James Higbie was born in Michigan and educated at Denison University (Granville, Ohio) and at the University of Hawaii. He has taught and trained teachers in Sierra Leone, Hawaii, Thailand, and Laos. This is his second book on the Thai language. His first, *Essential Thai*, was published in Bangkok in 1997.

Copyright© 1999 James Higbie

Second printing, 2001.

ISBN 0-7818-0774-3

For information, address:
HIPPOCRENE BOOKS, INC.
171 Madison Avenue
New York, NY 10016

Printed in the United States of America.

CONTENTS

INTRODUCTION

Many people who visit or work in Thailand learn to speak Thai. This is partly from necessity, as few Thais speak English, but also because of some positive aspects of Thai culture. In Thailand it's customary to talk to strangers. People will start talking to you everywhere you go, and will always be happy if you try to speak their language. The Thai language itself is easy and you can start having conversations with people right away.

Thai belongs to the Tai language family, a group of related languages spoken in Thailand, Laos, Burma (by the Shan ethnic group), and northern Vietnam and southern China (by minority ethnic groups). The dialect spoken in Bangkok and surrounding areas is called Central Thai. It's the official language of Thailand and the language in this book. There are three other main Tai languages spoken in Thailand: Southern Thai, Northern Thai, and Laotian, called Northeastern Thai or *Ee-san* in Thailand. There are also local varieties of each language. These Tai dialects differ from each other mainly by vocabulary and are not mutually intelligible. It would take a person from

Bangkok some time to be able to speak Northern Thai or another member of the Tai language family well.

Central Thai is the language of government, media, and education and is spoken throughout the country. People outside of central Thailand usually use their local language at home but switch to Central Thai when they're in school or doing business. The many smaller ethnic groups who live in Thailand also learn to speak and read Central Thai in school.

Thai, like Vietnamese and the Chinese languages, is a tonal language. Learning to say the tones isn't easy and you need a good memory in order to remember both the letter pronunciation and the tone of every word. People often cut corners by ignoring the tones. This isn't a problem at first because Thai people won't expect perfect pronunciation from a beginner and will usually be able to figure out what you're trying to say. However, if you want to speak Thai well, you should learn the tones, and some words definitely need their tones to be understood, such as "five" (*ha*) which has a falling tone and "pork" (*moo*) which needs a rising tone.

Thai words usually have only one syllable. The multi-syllable words in Thai usually concern government, academic subjects, or religion and came to the language through Sanskrit, the classical Indian language. When a new word is needed in Thai, such as a word for "fax", it's taken from Sanskrit. You may notice a similarity between some high level Thai words and equivalent English words. This arose through a historical connection between Greek and Latin and the ancient languages of central Asia and India. Many words are also borrowed from English.

The written form of Thai was also taken from Sanskrit. It's read phonetically from left to right like English but has more letters than English, for example four different letters for "s". Unlike English, the spelling of a word in Thai usually reflects its exact pronunciation; learning to read can help you with your pronunciation.

As you learn Thai you'll see how concise a language it is. English is often praised for its large vocabulary. Thai is the opposite, with a minimum of basic words and prefixes that are combined to form more complex meanings. The sentence structure is also simple, following the meaning of the sentence word by word. Thai does have grammar but it's a grammar of word order, not of changes in word form for tense or position.

Thai like all languages has variations in degree of correctness and formality. "R", for example, is almost always pronounced "l" informally but on TV, in Thai language classes, and in polite situations people will try to pronounce "r" correctly. Vocabulary can also change and there are formal and informal variations for "eat", "drink", and many other words. As in English, people tend to use high-level vocabulary and more complicated sentence structure in formal situations.

One aspect of Thai culture evident from the language is the emphasis on politeness. Using polite forms of language in Thai shouldn't be thought of as demeaning to the speaker. In its best form the politeness in Thai reflects mutual respect, not a hierarchical social structure. Conversations in

Thailand tend to be pleasant and fun. Controversial subjects aren't brought up and people usually don't speak sarcastically or abusively. In fact, talking loudly or rudely is taken seriously in Thailand and should be avoided.

Westerners usually find the spontaneous, relaxed atmosphere of the country very appealing and this is another reason why many people learn to speak Thai. It's an enjoyable place to travel and live in, and Thai people are so friendly you want to be able to talk to everyone you meet.

PRONUNCIATION

Before reading any of the Thai words in this book you should be aware of four main differences between the spelling system used here and English. First, the letter *a* is pronounced "ah" as in "father", so the word for "house", *ban,* is pronounced "bahn". Secondly words with "o" like *hot* are pronounced "hote". *Rot* is "rote", and *mot* is "mote". Next, *ph* isn't "f" but "p" as in English, and finally *th* is pronounced "t", not as "th" in English. The single letters *t* and *p* are used to represent hard consonant sounds that aren't common in English.

Tones and vowel length - People learning Thai often feel that the pronunciation is one of the hardest things about the language. Speakers of western languages are used to using tones (or inflection) to express emotions and differences in meaning. In Thai the tone is as much a part of a word's pronunciation as its letter sounds.

Pronunciation in Thai varies not only by tone but by the length of the vowel sound. Thai words have either a long vowel length, with the pronunciation drawn out, or a short vowel length with the word pronounced quickly. In this book short vowel-length words are marked with an asterisk.

In all, there can be ten different pronunciations for every "word": the five tones each with two vowel lengths (although no Thai "word" has meanings for all ten). Try to listen to a Thai speaker pronounce these examples.

mid tone - Your normal speaking voice.

mid-short	yang	still/yet
mid-long	yang	rubber

low tone - Lower than your normal sound.

low-short	gae	undo
low-long	gae	old

falling tone - Start high and go down to a normal, mid sound.

falling-short	kao	enter
falling-long	kao	rice

high tone - Higher than your normal voice.

high-short	mai	interrogative
high-long	mai	wood

rising tone - Start low and go up to a mid tone.

rising-short	laiŋ	flow
rising-long	laiŋ	a lot

12

Consonants - Two consonant sounds may be difficult for English speakers. These are the **hard t** and **hard p**. The first is a cross between "t" and "d" like the "t" in "sixty" and the second a cross between "p" and "b". Following is a list of consonant letters whose sounds are different from those in English:

p	a hard p/b sound
ph	pronounced as "p" in English
t	a hard t/d sound
th	pronounced as "t" in English
g	has a hard sound, between "g" and "k"
j	a harder sound than in English
ng	the same as in English but used at the beginning of words
r	slightly rolled, although "r" is usually pronounced as "l" in colloquial Thai

Vowels -

a	as in "father"
ay	"ay" as in "say" or "eh" as in "bet"
ae	as in "cat"
e	as in "met"
ee	as in "see"
i	as in "bit"
ai	as in "Thai"
aw	ao in "oaw"
o	as in "coat"
u	as in "but"
oo	as in "boot"
eu	as in the American pronunciation of "good"
euh	as in the British pronunciation of "Bert"

13

Vowel combinations - These combine two or more vowel sounds into one smooth sound. Some of them aren't used in English.

ao	ah + oh, as in "how"
oi	aw + ee
oy	oh + ee, as in "Chloe"
eo	ay + oh, as in "mayo"
aeo	ae + oh
ia	ee + uh, as in "Pia"
io	ee + oh as in "Leo"
iu	ee + oo, as in "mew"
ua	oo + uh, as in "Kalua"
ui	oo + ee, as in "Louie"
uay	oo + ay + ée, this sound ends with a very short "ée"
eua	eu + uh
euy	euh + ee
euay	eua + ay + ée

Colloquial pronunciation - Following are some characteristics of informal Thai pronunciation:

-r as l - "R" is almost always pronounced as "l". You may hear "hotel" pronounced *long-laem* instead of *rong-raem* and "vehicle" pronounced *lot* ("lote") instead of *rot* ("rote").

-r/l omitted - "R" or "l" is left out when it's the second sound. *Gra-pao* ("suitcase") becomes *ga-pao* and *pla* ("fish") is *pa*.

-Final sound/first syllable - In words like *kot-sa-na* ("advertisement) and *phan-ra-ya* ("wife") the "t" and "n" at the end of the first syllable isn't pronounced.

BASIC GRAMMAR

Thais like to speak politely and the Thai language has two words, *ka* for women and *krup* for men, that are put at the end of questions, responses and statements to make them sound more polite. *Ka* and *krup* are also used to answer "yes" politely. It's important to include these words when you're first talking to someone you don't know. They can be dropped after a few sentences in informal conversation. *Krup* has a single pronunciation but *ka* has three different pronunciations depending on how it's being used.

polite word, women

questions	k̄a᷄
responses/statements	k̠a᷄
emphasis	k̄a᷇

polite word, men

all uses	k̄ru̅p᷄

Pronouns vary according to the formality of the occasion and the relationship of the speakers. The following are common in everyday speech. Note that in Thai the same word is both "I" and "me", "she" and "her", etc.

I, female (informal)	chan
I, male (general)	phom̧
you	koon
she/he/they	kao
we	rao
it	mun

Phuak is a pluralizer that can be included with "we" and "they" for formality or to clarify or emphasize plurality.

| we | phuak̀ rao |
| they | phuak̀ kao |

Relationship terms are commonly used in the place of "you" and "I". People who aren't actually related can be addressed as "aunt", "uncle", "grandmother", etc. The following two terms are used among people from the same generation.

| younger person | nawng |
| older person | phee |

Phee ("older person") and *koon* ("you") may be put before peoples' first names to emphasize respect. *Phee* denotes people who are older than you but from the same generation. Calling an older colleague *Phee Daeng* or *Phee Noi* is a way of showing respect. *Koon* before the first name (*Koon John*) is common in formal situations, such as in offices and on the phone. When this word is written in English it's usually spelled *khun*. Several other common pronouns you may hear are:

noo̯	"I" for children (means "mouse")
theuh	intimate for "I", "you", "he", "she"
dee-chan̯	"I" for women, formal

"To be" isn't used with adjectives. Feelings or descriptive words are put right after the subject of the sentence. *Mai* (with a falling tone) makes the meaning negative. It's put before the adjective (or verb). "Hungry" in the first sentence is literally "hungry for rice".

I'm hungry. (said by a man)	Phom̯ hiu̯-kao.
I'm not well. (said by a woman)	Chan mai sa-bai.
Daeng is beautiful.	Daeng suay̯.

Adjectives and proper names go after nouns. There is no "a", "the", or plural form. All colors have the word *see* (meaning "color") before them.

a big room	hawng̯ yai
the Erawan Hotel	rong-raem Ay-ra-wan
Thai person/people	kon Thai
a white shirt ("shirt-color-white")	seua̯ see̯ kao̯

"To be" is used to link nouns only. There are two words for "to be" - *pen* and *keu*. The first is more common, *keu* being used only to link two things that are exact equivalents. *Keu* is also optional in informal speech (and in this example it's in parentheses). The negative is made with *mai chai*. *Pen* and *keu* aren't included in the negative.

He's Chinese.	Kao pen kon Jeen.
She's not Japanese.	Kao mai chai kon Yee-poon.
This is French wine.	Nee (keu) lao Fa-rang-set.
This isn't a big bottle.	Nee mai chai kuat yai.

Yes/no questions are formed by putting *mai* (pronounced high/short) at the end of statements. Simple questions aren't answered with "yes" or "no" but by repeating the adjective or verb for "yes" or putting the negative word *mai* (falling/short) before it for "no". Pronouns "you" and "I" aren't needed in informal conversation if it's understood who you're talking about. It's possible to leave them out of many of the examples in this book. "It" (*mun*) is usually omitted and is included only to emphasize the object or topic you're talking about. For "It's good" just say one word - *dee*. The use of pronouns and longer sentences are in general more polite and formal.

Are you hungry?	Koon hiu-kao mai?
(omit "you")	Hiu-kao mai?
Yes.	Hiu.
No.	Mai hiu.
Is it good?	Dee mai?
Yes./It's good.	Dee.
No./It's not good.	Mai dee.
Is it beautiful?	Suay mai?

Yes./It's beautiful.	Suay).
No./It's not beautiful.	Mai suay).
Are you having fun?	Sa-nook mai?
Yes./I'm having fun.	Sa-nook.
No./I'm not having fun.	Mai sa-nook.
Is it expensive?	Phaeng mai?
Yes./It's expensive.	Phaeng.
No./It's not expensive.	Mai phaeng.

The following words and phrases are also used for "yes" and "no".

Yes (polite for men)	krup
Yes (polite for women)	ka
Yes (informal)	euh, uh, ah, mm
Yes, that's right	chai
No, that's not right	mai chai

Two more ways to form questions are to put *reu plao* ("or not") or *reuh* (inflected question) at the end.

Are you going or not?	Pai reu plao?
Yes./No.	Pai./Mai pai.
Do you want it?	Ao reu plao?
Yes./No.	Ao./Mai ao.
You're going?	Pai reuh)?
You're not going?	Mai pai reuh)?

19

A final way to form questions is with *chai mai* as a tag question. These questions are answered with *chai* for "yes" and *mai chai* for "no".

You're American, aren't you?	Koon pen kon A-may-ree-ga, chai mai?
Yes.	Chai.
No. I'm Canadian. (said by a man)	Mai chai. Phomɟ pen kon Kae-na-da.

Following are examples of common **statements, negatives, and questions** using adjectives and verbs. **Sentences with the female pronoun *chan* are marked (f) and those with the male pronoun *phom* are marked (m).**

Thai food is delicious.	A-hanɟ Thai a-roi.
Thai food isn't delicious.	A-hanɟ Thai mai a-roi.
Is Thai food delicious?	A-hanɟ Thai a-roi mai?
Yes./No.	A-roi./Mai a-roi.
Ko Chang is beautiful.	Gaw Chang suayɟ.
Ko Chang isn't beautiful.	Gaw Chang mai suayɟ.
Is Ko Chang beautiful?	Gaw Chang suayɟ mai?
Yes./No.	Suayɟ./Mai suayɟ.
I'm going to Phuket. (f)	Chan pai Phoo-get.
I'm not going to Phuket. (f)	Chan mai pai Phoo-get.
Are you going to Phuket?	Pai Phoo-get mai?
Yes./No.	Pai./Mai pai.
I like Thai food. (m)	Phomɟ chawp a-hanɟ Thai.
I don't like Thai food. (m)	Phomɟ mai chawp a-

	haŋ Thai.
Do you like Thai food?	Koon chawp a-haŋ Thai mai?
Yes./No.	Chawp./Mai chawp.
I have ice./There's ice.	Mee nam-kaeŋɟ.
I don't have ice./There's no ice.	Mai mee nam-kaeŋɟ.
Do you have ice?/Is there ice?	Mee nam-kaeŋɟ mai?
Yes./No.	Mee./Mai mee.

"This" and "that" are put after nouns informally. In formal/correct Thai the "classifier" must be included. See the explanation for classifiers below.

this/that	nee/nan
This hotel is good.	Rong-raem nee dee.
That hotel isn't good.	Rong-raem nan mai dee.
Is this restaurant expensive?	Ran-a-haŋ nee phaeng mai?
Yes, it's expensive.	Phaeng.

Add *mak* for **"very"** and *leuy* for **"not at all"**.

| Ko Samet is very beautiful. | Gaw Sa-met suayɟ mak. |
| Chonburi isn't beautiful at all. | Chon-boo-ree mai suayɟ leuy. |

21

Add *laeo* ("already") for an **action or state that's completed**.

That's enough.	Phaw laeo.
I'm full.	Im laeo.
He's come already.	Kao ma laeo.
The water's gone.	Nam mot laeo.
I'm finished./It's finished.	Set laeo.

Put *gwa* after adjectives for the **comparative** ("bigger") and *thee-soot* for the superlative ("the biggest").

This restaurant is better.	Ran-a-hanɟ nee dee gwa.
Bangkok is bigger than Chiang Mai.	Groong-thayp yai gwa Chiang Mai.
Ko Phi Phi is the most beautiful.	Gaw Phee-Phee suayɟ thee-soot.

Tenses aren't complicated. Verbs have one form which can refer to any time - past, present, or future. There are four words that may be included to emphasize or clarify the meaning. With the present continuous ("I'm eating") *gam-lang* can be added to emphasize that the action is continuous and *yoo* can be added to show that the state exists. For the future, *ja* is put before verbs and for the negative past *dai* is put between *mai* ("not") and the verb.

I'm studying Thai. (f)	Chan rian pha-saɟ Thai.
(emphasize continuous)	Chan gam-lang rian pha-saɟ Thai.

(emphasize the state)	Chan rian pha-saj Thai yoo.
I'm going to Ayuthaya. (m)	Phomj ja pai A-yoot-tha-ya.
I'm not going to Korat. (m)	Phomj mai pai Ko-rat.
He went swimming.	Kao pai wai-nam.
I didn't go to Ubon. (m)	Phomj mai dai pai Oo-bon.

Questions and statements with **"yet" and "still"** are formed as follows:

yet/still	yang
Has John gone yet?	John pai reu yang?
Yes.	Pai laeo.
No.	Yang.
John's gone already.	John pai laeo.
John hasn't gone yet.	John yang mai dai pai.
John isn't going yet.	John yang mai pai.
John's still at home.	John yang yoo ban.

Sentences with **auxillary verbs** have the words strung together in a simple order.

want to	yak
I want to go shopping. (f)	Chan yak pai seu kawngj.
I don't want to go. (m)	Phomj mai yak pai.
have to	tawng
I have to go to the bank. (f)	Chan tawng pai tha-na-kan.

like/like to	chawp
I like to listen to music. (m)	Phom chawp fang phlayng.
I don't like to drink. (f)	Chan mai chawp gin lao.
might	at ja
I might go to Chiang Rai. (m)	Phom at ja pai Chiang Rai.
have ever	keuy
Have you ever gone to Hua Hin?	Koon keuy pai Hua Hin mai?
Yes.	Keuy.
No, never.	Mai keuy.
I've gone to Hua Hin. (f)	Chan keuy pai Hua Hin.
I've never gone to Hua Hin. (m)	Phom mai keuy pai Hua Hin.

"Can" is either *dai* or *pen*. *Dai* is used for any meaning of "can" (availability, permission, ability) while *pen* is used for ability only. *Pen* is commonly used to ask if someone is "able" to eat certain kinds of food. "Can" and "can't" are put at the end of sentences.

Can you go?	Pai dai mai?
Yes.	Dai.
No.	Mai dai.
I can go. (m)	Phom pai dai.
I can't go. (m)	Phom pai mai dai.

24

Can you eat Thai food?	Gin a-han̦ Thai pen mai?
Yes./No.	Pen./Mai pen.

For the **possessive** put the pronoun or name of the owner after the object, with the word *kawng* optionally between them. "Whose", "mine", "yours", etc., include *kawng*. The possessive isn't needed in phrases like "my mother" in the last example.

Where's John's house?	Ban (kawng̦) John yoo thee-nai̦?
It's in Bangkok.	Yoo Groong-thayp.
who	krai
whose?	kawng̦ krai?
Whose is this?	Un nee kawng̦ krai?
my/mine/It's mine. (f)	kawng̦ chan
my/mine/It's mine. (m)	kawng̦ phom̦
It's his/hers	kawng̦ kao
It's John's.	kawng̦ John
I live with my mother. (f)	Chan yoo gap mae.

Classifiers are used in a variety of patterns, among them numbers, how many, this/that, which, and each. They are the one area of Thai grammar considered difficult, but their use is similar to the way containers are counted and referred to in English. The first example shows how bottles of drinks are counted with the word "bottle" as the classifier.

bottle/classifier for things in bottles	kuat
water	nam
one	neung
one bottle of water ("water-one-bottle")	nam neung kuat
I'd like one bottle of beer.	Kawɹ nam neung kuat.

All objects in Thai have classifiers, not just containers. Here shirts are referred to with the classifier for clothing - *tua*.

shirt	seua
classifier for clothing	tua
two	sawngɹ
two shirts	seua sawngɹ tua
I have two shirts. (f)	Chan mee seua sawngɹ tua.
how many	gee (classifier)
how many shirts?	seua gee tua?
buy	seu
How many shirts did you buy?	Koon seu seua gee tua?
three	samɹ
I bought three shirts. (m)	Phomɹ seu seua samɹ tua.
which	(classifier) naiɹ
which shirt?	seua tua naiɹ?
Which shirt do you like?	Koon chawp seua tua naiɹ?

(omit "shirt")	Kŏon chawp tua naiɉ?
this	nee
this shirt	seua tua nee, tua nee
I like this shirt. (m)	Phŏmɉ chawp tua nee.

Following is a list of common classifiers:

boats	lum
books	lem
bottles	kuat
buildings	langɉ
clothes/furniture	tua
glasses of drinks	gaeo
objects in general	un
pairs of things	koo
people	kon
pieces of things	chin
places	thee, haeng
plates of food	jan
round objects	look
sets of things	choot
small objects	bai
tapes	ta-lap, muan
things in strands	sen
trees/plants	ton
vehicles	kun

For **requests** put *chuay* ("help") at the beginning and *noi* ("a little") or *duay* ("also") at the end. *Ka* and *krup* can also be included at the end. For "don't" use *ya* or *mai tawng*. The first is stronger and the second means "you don't have to". The particle *na* is put at the end of these requests with "don't". It's a common word in Thai and means "mind you", "isn't it?", or "OK?". Use *kaw* when asking to do an action as in the last sentence.

Please open the window.	Chuay peuht na-tang noi.
Don't open the door!	Ya peuht pra-too, na.
You don't have to close the door.	Mai tawng pit pra-too, na.
May I take your picture?	KawɈ thai roop koon dai mai?

Common **prepositions** are as follows:

about - think/dream	theungɈ
I thought about you./I missed you. (m)	PhomɈ kit theungɈ koon.
about/concerned with	gio-gap
What field do you study?	Rian gio-gap a-rai?
about/on the subject of	reuang
What are you talking about?	Koon kui reuang a-rai?
for (someone)	hai, samɈ-rap
This is for you.	Un nee hai koon.
	Un nee samɈ-rap koon.
I bought it for you. (f)	Chan seu hai koon.
from	jak
He comes from Myanmar.	Kao ma jak Pha-ma.

with	gap
I came with my older brother. (m)	Phomj ma gap phee-chai.
at	thee
I stay at a hotel. (f)	Chan phak thee rong-raem.
at/stay at	yoo, yoo thee
Noi is at home.	Noi yoo (thee) ban.
Lek is in Chiang Mai.	Lek yoo (thee) Chiang Mai.
in	nai
She's in the room.	Kao yoo nai hawng.

Common **conjunctions** are as follows:

that/which/who	thee
The shirt that you bought is very nice.	Seua thee koon seu suayj mak.
The person who works there is named Maeo.	Kon thee tham-ngan thee-nan cheu Maeo.
that - said/thought	wa
What did she say?	Kao phoot wa a-rai?
She said that she wasn't coming.	Kao phoot wa kao mai ma.
I think he's coming today. (m)	Phomj kit wa kao ja ma wan-nee.
and/with	gap
I'm going to Pattaya and Ko Chang.	Chan ja pai Phat-tha-ya gap Gaw Chang.

and/then	laeo, laeo gaw
I'm going shopping then I'm going to eat. (m)	Phom ja pai seu kawng laeo pai gin kao.
but	tae
I'm going but he isn't. (f)	Chan ja pai tae kao mai pai.
or	reu
Are you going to Chiang Mai or Chiang Rai?	Koon ja pai Chiang Mai reu Chiang Rai?
if	tha
If I have time I'll go to Ko Tao. (m)	Tha mee way-la phom ja pai Gaw Tao.

THAI-ENGLISH DICTIONARY

This dictionary contains basic vocabulary and also the main function words and prefixes of Thai, words whose basic meanings are combined to form more complex vocabulary and phrases. Also included are some Thai homonyms, words whose pronunciations differ only by tone or vowel length. Note that in Thai, nouns are the same whether singular or plural. Only the singular form is given in the English translation. Also, some Thai words have several meanings, for example, *pai* (with a mid tone/short vowel length) can mean both "go" and "too", as in "too hot".

A

a̱b-nam	bathe, take a bath
a-deet	the past
aep (followed by verb)	do surreptitiously
aep doo	peek at
a-gat	air, weather, climate

31

a-hanɉ	food
an	read
a-na-kot	future
a-noo-yat	permit, allow, permission
an-ta-rai	dangerous
ao	want, take
a-rai	what, anything, something, whatever
a-roi	delicious
a-rom	mood, emotion(s)
at ja (verb)	might
a-thit	week
awk	go out, put forth
awn	young, weak (taste), light (colors)
ayng	oneself
a-yoo	age

B

baeng	share, divide
baeng	bank note
baep	style, kind, design, as, like
bai	leaf, sail, classifier for small objects
bai, tawn bai	early afternoon
ban	house, home
ban nawk	countryside

bang	thin (for objects)
bang (classifier)	some
bang kòn	some people
bang-thee	maybe, sometimes
bang	some, somewhat
ban-ya-gat	atmosphere
bao	light (opp. heavy), soft (opp. loud)
bawk	tell
baw-ree-gan	service, to serve
baw-ree-sat	company
baw-ree-soot	innocent, pure
beua	bored, tired of
bin	bill
bin	fly (v)
bon	on, on top of, above
bon	complain
bo-ran	ancient, antique, traditional

Ch

cha	slow, slowly, late
châi	yes, that's right
chai	use
chai-daen	border
cha-lat	intelligent
chan	I, me (for women)
chan	class, level, grade
chang	weigh

33

chang	mechanic, an expert at
chang	elephant
chao	inhabitant of
chao	rent
chao, tawn chao	morning
chat	nation, nationality
chat	clear, clearly
chawp	like, like to
cheet	spray, inject
cheu	name, first name
cheua	believe, sure
cheuŋ-cheuŋ	indifferent, impassive
chin	accustomed to
chin	piece
chok	luck
chok	hit, punch, box
chon	bump, crash into
chon-na-bot	countryside
choot	set, suit, uniform
chuan	invite
chuang	period, duration
chuay	help

D

dai	thread, string (cotton)
dai	can, get (also used as past tense marker)
dai rap	receive
dai yin	hear

dam, seej dam	black
dang	loud, noisy, famous
dao	star, planet
dawk-mai	flower
dee	good
dee gwa	better, would be better, would rather
dee-jai	happy, glad
dee keun	improved
dee thee-soot	the best
dek	child, young person
deuan	month
deuhm	original, former, previous, first
deuhn	walk
deuhn-thang	travel (v)
deuk	late (at night)
deum	drink
din	soil
dio	single, sole, only
dio-gan	one and the same
dioj	in a moment
dioj-nee	right now
dip	raw
don	touch, hit, come in contact with (also used as passive voice marker)
don-tree	music
doo	look, look at, seems

doo <u>meuan</u>ɲ	looks like, seems like
doo <u>nang</u>ɲ	see a movie
doo-lae	take care of
<u>duan</u>	express, urgent
duang	classifier for stamps, sources of light
<u>duay</u>	also, too
<u>duay</u>-gàn	together

E

<u>eeg</u>	more, again, in addition, other
<u>eun</u>	other, another (some other, not this one)

F

fa	sky
<u>fa</u>ɲ	wall (of a room)
<u>fa</u>ɲ	lid, top
faen	boyfriend, girlfriend, husband, wife
fai	fire, electricity
<u>fak</u>	deposit, entrust
fang	listen (to)
fangɲ	bury
fao	guard, take care of
<u>feuk</u>	train (v), practice
<u>fon</u>ɲ	rain (v)
<u>foon</u>	dust

fun	tooth
funj	dream (v)

G

gae	open, undo
gae	old (for living things), dark (colors), strong (coffee/tea)
gae	correct, solve, remedy
gaeo	glass (drinking), crystal
gam-lang	power, force, energy
gam-lang-jai	will power, spirit
gam-not	limit, set, stipulate, schedule
gan	each other
gan	affairs of, matters of (prefix)
gan meuang	politics
gao	old (for objects), former
gao	nine
gap	with, and
gaw	island
gaw sang	construction work
gaw	still, also, subsequently (linking/hypothetical)
gaw dai	would be alright
gawn	first (before something else), previous

gawn	lump, classifier for lump-shaped objects
gee (classifier)	how many
gee-la	sports
geng	expertly, well, good at
gep	collect, pick up, keep
gep wai	keep, save
geuap	almost, nearly, about
geuhn	over, to exceed, in excess
geuhn pai	too (as in "too hot")
geuht	born, happen, originate
gin	eat, drink (informal)
gin lao	drink liquor
gin ya	take medicine
gio	concern, be concerned with, related to
gio-gap	about, concerning
glai	far
glai	near, just about to
glang	center, middle, central
glap	go back, return, turn back
glap ban	go home
glap ma	come back
glap pai	go back
glawng	drum
glawng	box, carton
glawng thai roop	camera
gliat	hate

gloom	group (of people)
glua	afraid
go-hòk	lie, tell a lie (to)
gong	cheat (v)
goon-jae	key, wrench (tool)
gra-dat	paper
gra-jòk	window glass, mirror
gra-paoɹ	suitcase, purse, pocket
gra-pawngɹ	can (tin can)
gwa	more than
gwang	deer
gwang	wide

H

ha	five
haɹ	look for
haeng	place, classifier for places
haeng	dry
hai	give, let, allow, cause, have/make (someone do something)
haiɹ	gone, disappeared, missing
hàk	break (in two)
ham	don't, prohibit
hang	be at a distance
hawmɹ	nice-smelling, to kiss (both adj and verb)

hawnḡ	room
henj	see, notice
hiu	carry (something with a handle)
hiuʝ	hungry
hok	six
hoon	shape
hoon̄	stock, share
huaʝ	head
huay	stream
huayʝ	lottery

I

im	full (from eating)

J

ja	will, would
jai	heart/mind (figurative)
jai-dee	glad, happy
jai-rawn	hot-tempered, impulsive, anxious
jai	pay (v)
jak	from, go away (from)
jam	remember
jam-gat	limit, limited
jam-nuan	quantity, amount
jam-pen	must, be necessary
jang	extremely

jang	hire
jao kawng	owner (of)
jao na-thee	official (person)
jap	touch, catch, arrest, hold
jat	arrange, put in order, prepare
jat	intense, strong
jawng	reserve (rooms/seats)
jawng	stare (at)
jawt	park, stop (a vehicle)
jeep	flirt with, woo
jep	hurt, be injured
jet	seven
jeuh	meet, run into unexpectedly, find
jeut	bland, unseasoned
jing	true, real
jing-jai	sincere
jon	poor, until, up to the point of/that
jon	thief
joop	kiss
joot	point, spot, decimal point, period
joot	ignite, light (a fire)
jop	finish, end (an action of defined duration)
jot-mai	letter

K

ka	galanga (a type of ginger)
ka	kill
ka	charge for, fee, value
ka chao	rent money
kaj	leg
ka kaij	sell, engage in trade
kae	only (a small amount), to the extent of, level
kaek	guest (also "Indian" or "Muslim")
kaeng, kaeng-kunj	race, compete
kaengj	hard (opp. soft)
kaengj-raeng	strong (physically)
kai	egg
kai	fever
kaij	sell
kam	word
kam, tawn kam	evening
kam	cross, go across
ka-moy	steal
ka-na	period (of time)
ka-nat	size, extent, magnitude
kang	chin
kang	side, beside
kang keun	stay overnight
ka-nomj	snack, dessert
kao	news

kao	enter, go in
kao-jai	understand
kao	rice
kao	he, she, they
kaoɟ	white
kàp	drive
kat	torn, break in two
kat	miss, lack, missing
kaw	neck, throat
kaw	joint, node, point (on a list) (also a prefix for worded content)
kaw-moon	information
kawɟ	ask for, request, beg
kawɟ-thot	excuse me, apologize
kawngɟ	thing, object, material (also used to denote possession)
kawngɟ-kwanɟ	present, gift
kee	ride
kee	excrement
kee	characterized by (prefix for describing people)
kee ai	shy
kem	salt, salty, salted
kemɟ	needle
keu	to be (also the phrase "that is to say")
keun	return (something)

43

keun	up, go up, rise, increase
keun-nee	this evening, tonight
keuy	have ever, used to
kianj	write, draw
kit	think, calculate
klai	similar to, resembles
klawng	canal
klawng	do (an action) well, (speak) fluently
koi	wait, wait for
koi	gradually, gently
kom	sharp
komj	bitter
kon	person, people, classifier for people
kong ja (verb)	probably
koo	pair
koom ka	worth it
koon	you, value, virtue
koon-na-phap	quality
kop	be friends with
kot-sa-na	advertisement, advertise
krai	who, anyone, whoever
krang	time, occasion
kreuang	machine, instrument, apparatus
kreung	half
krop	complete, everything is

	there
kuan jǎ (verb)	should
kŭi	talk, converse, chat
kŭn	itch, itchy
kŭn	classifier for vehicles
kwaj	right (side)
kwam	prefix used to form nouns
kwam-maij	meaning
kwam-rák	love (n)
kwam-rèo	speed
kwam-sòok	happiness

L

la	leave, take one's leave
la awk	quit (a job)
lǎ	each, per
lae	and (formal/written)
laek	trade, swap
laeo	already, then, and
laeo gaw	then, and
laeo tae	depends on
laí	pattern, striped
lǎi	shoulder
laî	to chase (out/away)
laî awk	fire (from a job)
laij	flow
laij (classifier)	a lot, many
làm-bak	a bother, difficult, hard

45

la̅ng	below, under
la̅ng	wash
láng̖	classifier for buildings
la̅ng̖	back, behind
la̅ng̖-jak	after
Lao	Laotian
la̅o̖	liquor, whisky
la̅o̖	tell, relate a story
láp	sleep, be asleep
law	handsome
la̅w	wheel
lawng	try, test out
lawt	tube, drinking straw
le̅k	number (used in phrases)
le̅k	little (in size)
le̅m	volume, classifier for books, carts
le̅n	play, do without a serious purpose
le̅uhk	quit, stop, be through
leum	forget
leuy	completely, utterly, past a place, therefore (this word has many uses)
li̅ang	raise, pay for, feed
li̅o	turn (a corner)
lo	kilogram
lo̖	dozen

lok	world, the earth
lom	wind (blowing)
lom	fall over
long	go down, descend
longɹ	go astray, become lost
look	child (of your own) (also a classifier for ball-shaped objects)
look keun	stand up, get up
lot	reduce, decrease
luangɹ	official, royal

M

ma	come
ma	horse
maɹ	dog
mae	mother
mae-nam	river
mai	new, again (anew)
mai	burn, be burned
mai	no, not (negative)
mai keuy	have never
mai koi..	not very..
mai mee	there isn't, don't have
mai meuanɹ	different, not the same
mai	interrogative (used to form questions)
mai	wood
maiɹ, pha maiɹ	silk

47

maiɲ-kwam waˆ..	means
makˋ	very, a lot
maˋo	drunk, high
mawɟ	doctor
mee	have, there is, there exists
menɲˋ	bad-smelling
meua	when, used before past time phrases
meua-rai	when, whenever
meuanɟ	the same as, like
meuang	city, town, country
meuay	tired (physically)
meun	ten thousand
meut	dark (no light)
mia	wife (informal term)
mia noi	mistress
mooɟ	pig, pork
moo-ban	village
motˋ	all, all gone, used up
motˋ	ant
munˋ	it, oil, oily, rich (food), potato (this word has many uses)
mungˋ	somewhat (colloquial)

N

na	rice field, farm field
na	season

nâ	face, front, in front of
nâ ja (verb)	should
nâ	prefix meaning "worthy of"
nâ glua	frightening
nâ rák	cute
nae	sure, certain, surely
nai	in, inside
naij	where, which (after classifier)
nák	heavy, heavily
nâk	mythical serpent (a "naga")
nák	prefix meaning "a person who"
nák gee-la	athlete
na-lee-ga	clock, watch, o'clock
nam	lead, bring
nam	water, liquid
nan	a long time
nân	that/those (referring to an object)
nan	that ("that hotel")
nâng	sit
nangj	skin, leather, movie
nang-seuj	book, magazine
nang-seuj phim	newspaper
naoj	cold (feeling/weather)
náp-theuj	respect, believe in

na-thee	minute
na-thee	duties
nawk	outer, outside, foreign
nawk-jak	besides, unless, except
nawn	lie down, sleep
nee	this/these (referring to an object)
nee	this ("this shirt")
neej	run away (from)
nee-saij	behavior, manners, character
nee-yom	to like (something that's popular)
neua	meat
neuaj	north (of), above
neuay	tired
neung	one
noi	a little, somewhat (adverb)
noi	a little (amount)
noom	young man, young (to describe a man)
noom	soft (to the touch)
nuat	moustache
nuat	massage

Ng

ngai	easy, easily, simply
ngan	work, task, job, party,

	festival, fair
ngáoj	lonely
ngeuhn	money, silver
ngiap	quiet, quietly
ngóng	confused, perplexed
nguang nawn	sleepy

O

o-gat	chance, opportunity
ong-sáj	degrees (temperature)
òt	go without, starve

P

pa	forest, jungle
pâ	aunt
paeng	powder, flour
paet	eight
pái	go, too (as in "too hot")
pâi	sign (signboard)
pan-háj	problem
pá-tee-bàt	carry out, act, do, perform (a task)
pee	year
pen	to be, can/able to
peuht	open, turn on
pìt	close, turn off, cover
plae	translate, mean
plaek	strange

plao	blank, void, empty
plawm	fake, counterfeit
plian	change (v)
plook	wake someone up
plook	plant, raise (crops), build (houses)
pok-ga-tee	normal, as usual, usually
poo	crab
poo	paternal grandfather
praeng	brush (n/v)
pra-jam	regular, regularly, always, permanent
pra-man	about, approximately
pra-phay-nee	customs, traditions
pra-thet	country
prio	sour

Ph

pha, pha pai	take (someone to a place)
pha	cloth
pha tat	operate (on the body)
phaeng	expensive
phak	vegetables
phak	part, section, region
phak	stay, rest, period of time
phak-phawn	rest, relax

phak	political party
phan	thousand
phan	pass through, pass by
phao	tribe
phaoj	burn (do actively)
pha-saj	language
phat	stir-fry
phat	blow (wind/fan)
phat-tha-na	develop, improve
phaw	enough, adequately
phaw	father
phawmj	thin, emaciated
pha-ya-yam	try, make an effort
phee	title for older person
pheej	ghost
phee-set	special, specially
phet	hot, spicy
phet	sex, gender
phet	diamond
pheua	in case, as a contingency
pheua	in order to, so that, for the sake of
pheuan	friend, acquaintance
pheuhm	increase, add on
phit	wrong, different, guilty
phit, mee phit	poisonous
phlayng	song

phom	I/me (men), hair on the head
phoo-chai	man
phoo-kao	mountain
phoo-ying	woman
phoot	speak, talk, say
phop	meet
phra	monk, lord, god, title for sacred things
phra a-thit	sun
phra jan	moon
phraw wa	because
phrawm	ready, completed, at the same time

R

ra-bop	system
ra-dap	level (n)
raek	first (in a series), beginning
raeng	strength, power, force, strongly
rai	plantation, unit of land measurement
rai-gan	program, list
rai-ngan	report (n/v)
rak	love (v)
ra-ka	price
rak-sa	cure, treat, protect,

	convalesce
ran	shop, store
rao	we/us
rap	receive, pick up, catch
rap-phit-chawp	responsible (for)
rat	state (a state in the U.S.)
rat-tha-ban	government
raw	wait (for)
ra-wang	be careful
ra-wang	between, during
rawn	hot (temperature)
rawng	cry out, shout
rawng hai	cry
rawng phlayng	sing
rawp	go around, cycle, lap, surrounding
reo	fast, early, soon
reuj	or
reuang	about, subject, situation, story
reuay-reuay	continuously
reuhj	really?, oh?
reuhm	start, originate
riak	call, is called
rian	study, learn, go to school
riap-roi	in order, ready, well-mannered, neat
roi	hundred

rom	shade, umbrella
rong-rian	school
roo	hole
roo	know
roo-jak	know a person/place
roon	model, generation, age group, period
roop	picture, form, shape
roo-seuk	feel
rop-guan	bother, disturb
rot	taste, flavor
rot	vehicle, car
rot	to water (plants), sprinkle water on
ruam	put together, combine
ruam	do together, share, mutual
ruay	rich, wealthy

S

sa-at	clean
sa-bai	well, comfortable, easily
sa-daeng	show (v/n)
sa-duak	convenient
saenj	hundred thousand
sai	sand
sai	put in, put on, wear
sai	to, toward (formal)

sai	left (side)
saiɲ	late, late morning
saiɲ	route, channel
sak, mai sak	teak wood
sak	tattoo (v)
sak	wash, launder
sak	indefinite quantifier
saɲ-la	pavilion, hall
samɲ	three
sa-maiɲ	time period, age, era
sa-mat	able to (formal)
samɲ-rap	for, designated for, as for
sa-namɲ	field (sports/landing)
sang	order (v), give orders
sang	build
sa-nit	tight, tightly, completely, intimate
sa-nook	fun, enjoyable, enjoy
Saoɲ, wan Saoɲ	Saturday
saoɲ	girl, young (to describe a woman)
sap-da	week
sat	animal
sa-thaɲ-nee	station
sa-thanɲ-thee	place
sat-sa-naɲ	religion
sawm	fork
sawm	fix, repair

57

sawm	practice
sawn̂	hide
sawnɟ	teach, train
sawng	envelope, packet
sawngɟ	two
sawp	take a test
sayt-tha-git	economy
see	four
seeɟ	color, paint (n)
sen̂	line, strand, classifier for things in strands, roads
set	finished, finish, ready, completed
seu	buy
seua	mat
seuâ	shirt
seuâ phâ	clothes
seuaɟ	tiger
seuk-saɟ	study (at a high level)
seu-sat	honest
siaɟ	use, lose, waste, broken, spoiled, polluted
siaɟ-daî	unhappy (from losing something)
siaɟ-jai	unhappy, sorry
siangɟ	sound, noise, sound of
sing	a thing, things, something

sing	mythical lion
sing-waet-lawm	environment
sip	ten
soi	lane, side street, cut into small pieces
soi kaw	necklace
som-moot wa	suppose that
song	send
song-kram	war
song-sai wa	suspect that, wonder if
song-san	pity (v)
son-jai	interested (in)
soo	to (a place, formal)
soo	fight with, compete
sook	ripe, cooked until done
Sook, wan Sook	Friday
sook-ka-phap	health
soon	center, headquarters, zero
soong	tall, high
soop	smoke, draw on, pump
soo-phap	polite
soot-thai	last (of a sequence), final, previous
sot	fresh, uncooked
sot	single, unmarried
suan	part (of something)
suan mak	most, mostly, usually
suan	garden, park

suay	bad luck
suayȷ	beautiful
sun	shake, tremble
sun	short (in length)
sunȷ-ya	promise, contract

T

ta	eye(s), maternal grandmother
tae	but, only (one kind)
tae la̅..	each, every
taek	break, broken, shatter, burst, split, smashed
taek-tang	differ, be different
taeng	decorate
taeng-ngan	marry, be married
tai	die (to die)
tai	south (of), under, below
tak	expose to, exposed to
ta-lat	market
tam	follow, along
tam	low
tang	different, separate, differ
tang hak	separately, instead
tang pra-thet	foreign
tang-tang	various
tang	set up, establish

tang-tae	since
tat	cut (v)
taw	next, further, extend, toward, continue (used in phrases for "per")
ta-wan	sun (poetic/used in directions)
tawn	when, at (for time)
tawng	must, have to, should
tawng-gan	would like, need
tee	hit, beat, fight
tem	full, full of, whole
tia	short (in height)
tit	attach, attached to, connect, addicted
tok	fall, fall down, drop
ton	beginning, source, classifier for plants
ton-mai	tree, plant
too	compartment, cabinet
trong	straight, direct, directly
truat	inspect, examine
tua	body, classifier for clothes, furniture, animals
tuaj	ticket

Th

tha	spread on
tha	if
tha reua	pier
thae	genuine, real
thaen	substitute, replace, instead (of)
thaeo	near, around, row
tham	do, make, cause
tham hai	cause, make (someone do something)
tham	cave
tham	ask
tham-ma-chat	nature, natural
tham-ma-da	regular, ordinary, usually, regularly
tham-mai	why
tham-ngan	work (v)
than	on time, in time
than	eat (polite)
than	battery, charcoal
thang	way, means, route, road, direction
thang-mot	all, altogether
thang sawng	both (used before classifier)
thang	barrel, bucket
tha-non	road, street
thao, see thao	gray

thao	equal, the same (size, quantity)
thao-gan	equal to each other
thao-nan	only, just, only that
thao-rai	how much
thao	foot
that	stupa (Laotian)
thawng	gold
thawng	abdomen
thawt	take off
thawt	fried, deep-fried
thee	time, occasion
thee	place, at, that, which, who
thee-din	land (piece of land)
thee-naij	where, anywhere, wherever
thee-nee	here, this place
thee sawngj	second (number two)
theuj	hold, believe, consider as
theungj	arrive, reach to, up to
thiij	throw away, desert, abandon
thio	visit, travel, go out
thon	last (a long time), endure
thook	cheap, correct, touch, (also used as passive voice marker)

thook	each, every (prefix)
thook yang	every kind, everything
thoong	bag, sack
thoong na	farm fields (empty)
thua	throughout, all over

U

uan	fat, well-built
un	one, a thing, item
un nee	this one

W

wa	that (as in "I said that"), said, thought, planned
waen	ring (n)
waen ta	eyeglasses
wai	Thai greeting
wai	keep, save, put, leave
wai-jai	trust (v)
wai	can (physically)
wai-nam	swim
wai-roon	teenager
wan	day
wan	sweet
wang	put down (object)
wang	free, not busy, vacant
wang wa	hope that

wat	draw, paint (a picture)
wat	measure
wat	temple compound
wat-tha-na-tham	culture
way-la	time
wing	run
wi-thee	way, method, means
wong	circle, group, classifier for circular objects
woon-wai	busy with, confusing, in confusion

Y

ya	medicine
ya	don't
ya	divorce
ya	paternal grandfather
ya	grass
yae	awful, terrible
yaek	separate, go apart
yai	maternal grandmother
yai	big
yai	move (to live in another place)
yak	want to
yak	hard, difficult
yak	giant, ogre
yang	still, yet
yang	rubber

yang	kind, type, as
yang	barbecued
yang-ngai	how (informal), any way, however
yang-ngee	like this, this kind
yao	long (in length)
yat	relative
yawt	peak
yee-haw	brand
yen	cold, cool (things)
yeuh	a lot
yeum	borrow
yim	smile
yok	lift, raise, round (in boxing)
yoo	be at, live at
yoong	mosquito
yoong	confusing, entangled, involved, involve
yoot	stop

ENGLISH-THAI
DICTIONARY

A

a few	sawng‚ sam‚
a little	nit noi
a lot	mak, yeuh
able to	dai
abortion, to abort	tham thaeng
about/approximately	pra-man
about/concerning	gio-gap, reuang
accent (in speaking)	sam‚-niang
accident	oo-bat-tee-hayt
accustomed to	chin gap
act (v)	sa-daeng
add	buak
add/put in	teuhm
add up/put together	ruam
addicted (to)	tit
addictive drug	ya sayp-tit

adjust	pràp
administrate	baw-ree-hǎnɈ
advertisement,	kot-sà-na
advertise	(or ko-sà-na)
advise/recommend	nae-nam
afraid	glua
again	eeg
again/newly	mài
agency	ong-gan
agree (after negotiations)	tòk-longɈ
agree (with an opinion)	henɈ duay
agree/accept/yield	yawm
agriculture	ga-sàyt-sat
air	a-gàt
air, for tires	lom
air-conditioned	ae, pràp a-gàt
air conditioner	kreuang ae
air pollution	a-gàt siaɈ
airplane crash	kreuang bin tòk
alike/similar	klai-klai gàn
alike/the same	meuanɈ-gàn
all/altogether	thang-mòt
all gone/used up	mòt
allow	hài, a-noo-yàt
almost	geuap
alone	kon dio
alphabet	tua àk-sǎwnɈ
alright/adequate	phaw chai dài
alright/would be	gàw dài

alright	
also (in addition)	duay
also (the same)	meuanɉ-gàn
also (together)	duay-gàn
amount	jam-nuan
amphetamine	ya ba
analyze	wee-kráw
ancestors	ban-phà-boo-root
ancient	bo-ran
and (formal)	laé
and/then	laeo, laeo gaw
and/with	gàp
Angkor Wat	Na-kawn Wat
angry	gròt
angry (suddenly)	mo-hoɉ
announce	prà-gàt
another/more	eeg
another person (more)	eeg kon neung
another (some other)	eun
another person (not this one)	kon eun
another place	thee eun
answer (v)	lawp
antenna	saoɉ a-gàt
antique/antiques	kawngɉ gao
apply	sà-màk
appropriate	maw somɉ
approximately	prà-man
archeology	bo-ran-nà-ká-dee

area	baw-ree-wayn, kayt
argue	tha-law
arrange	jat
arrest	jap
art/the arts	sin-la-pa
ask	tham
ask for permission	kaw a-noo-yat
ask for something	kaw..
atmosphere/ambiance	ban-ya-gat
attach/attached to	tit
attack (a person)	tham-rai
attack/invade	book, book-rook

B

bachelor	chai sot
bachelor's degree	prin-ya tree
bad (person)	chua, rai
bad/awful	yae
bad/not good	mai dee
bad luck	suay, chok rai
bad mood	a-rom mai dee
bad-smelling	men
bag/sack	thoong
bag/suitcase/purse	gra-pao
bald	hua lan
bamboo (wood)	mai phai
banana tree	ton gluay
band (music)	wong don-tree

Bangkok	Groong-thayp
bargain (v)	taw
basket	ta-gra
bathe	ab-nam
bathroom/toilet	hawng-nam
battery, flashlight	than fai-chaij
battery, vehicle	baet-ta-ree
bay	ao
be	pen, keu (see pages 17-18)
be at	yoo
beach	hat sai, chai hat
beat/rythmn	jang-wa
beautiful	suayj
beautiful (for music)	phraw
beautiful/pretty	ngam
beg alms	kawj than
begin	reuhm
believe	cheua
believe in	nap-theuj
bell	ra-kang
besides	nawk-jak
best	doo thoo soot
better (than)	dee gwa
better/improved	dee keun
big	yai
birth control	koom gam-neuht
birthday	wan geuht
bite	gat

bitter	kom̌
black	seě dam
black market	ta-lat meut
bland/unseasoned	jeut
bless	uay-phawn
blessing (n)	phawn
blind	ta bawt
blow (wind/fan)	phat
blow (from the mouth)	pao
blue, dark blue	seě nam-ngeuhn
blue, light blue	seě fa
boil/boiled	tom
boil/is boiling	deuat
bomb (n)	ra-beuht
bomb/drop bombs	thing ra-beuht
book	nang-seǔ
border	chai-daen
bored	beua
boring	na beua
born	geuht
borrow	yeum
both	thang sawnǧ
both people	thang sawnǧ kon
both things	thang sawnǧ un
bother/a bother	lam-bak
bother/disturb	rop-guan
bothered (by)	ram-kan
box/carton	glawng

boyfriend	faen
brake	brayk
brand	yee-haw
break (from work)	phak
break (in two)	hak
break/shatter	taek
break up (relationship)	leuhk gan
breathe	hai-jai
bride	jao sao
bridegroom	jao bao
bring (a person)	pha ma
bring (an object)	ao ma
broken (in two)	hak
broken (not working)	sia
broken (shattered)	taek
broken-hearted	ok hak
brothel	sawng
brown	see nam-tan
brush (n/v)	praeng
brush your teeth	praeng fun
budget	ngop pra-man
build	sang
building	teuk
bullet	look peun
bump into	chon
burn (do actively)	phao
burn (is burning)	mai
bury	fang
but	tae

buy	seu
buy things/shop	seu kawngɹ

C

cage	grong
calculate	kit
calendar	pa-tee-thin
call (to a place - phone)	tho pai
call/is called	riak
camera	glawng thai roop
can (tin can)	gra-pawngɹ
can/able to	dai, pen
canal	klawng
candle	thian
capital city	meuang luangɹ
carry	hiu
carry/hold	theuɹ
cart	gwian
casket	heep sop
cassette (tape)	thayp
catch	jap
cause (n)	saɹ-hayt
cause to..	tham hai..
cave	tham
celebrate	cha-lawng
cement	poon
cemetery, Chinese	soo-sanɹ
cemetery, Thai	pa-cha
center/headquarters	soonɹ

center/middle	glang
centimeter	sen-ti-met, sen
century	sat-ta-wat
ceremony	phee-thee
chain	so
chance/opportunity	o-gat
change (v)	plian
change your mind	plian jai
channel (TV)	chawng
chapter	bot
characteristic(s)	lak-sa-na
charcoal	than
chase after	lai tam
cheap	thook
cheat (v)	gong
cheat/deceive	lawk, lawk luang
check/examine	truat
chemical	sang-kay-mee
chew	kio
chew betel	gin mak
choose	leuak
cigarette	boo-ree
cigarette lighter	fai chack
city/town	meuang
class/level	chan
clean (adj)	sa-at
clean (v)	tham kwam sa-at
clear/clearly	chat
climate/weather/air	a-gat

ENGLISH-THAI DICTIONARY

climb	peen
clock/watch	na-lee-ga
close (v)	pit
closed	pit laeo
cloth	pha
clothes/clothing	seua pha
coast/shore	fang tha-lay
cold, feeling/weather	nao
cold, things	yen
collect, as a hobby	sa-som
collect/pick up	gep
college/university	ma-ha wit-tha-ya-lai
colony	meuang keun, a-na-nee-kom
color	see
comb	wee
comb your hair	wee phom
come	ma
come back	glap ma
come from	ma jak
come in	kao ma
comfortable	sa-bai
commerce	gan ka
committee	ka-na gam-ma-gan
company/business	baw-ree-sat
compare	priap thiap
compass	kem thit
compete	kaeng, kaeng-kun
complain	bon

complete (includes everything that should be there)	krop
completed/finished	set laeo
complicated/detailed	la-iat
complicated/hard to understand	sup-sawn
computer	kawm-phiu-teuh
concentration	sa-ma-thee
concert	kawn-seuht
condition/state	sa-phap
condom	thoongj yang
confident	mun-jai
confirm	yeun-yan
confused	ngong
confusing	sup-sonj
consciousness	sa-tee
consideration for others	grayng-jai
consonant (letter)	pha-yan-cha-na
constitution (of gov't)	rat-tha-tham-ma-noon
consult	preuk-saj
contact	tit-taw
contest	pra-guat
continuously	reuay-reuay
contract	sunj-ya
control/supervise	kuap-koom, koom
convenient	sa-duak
cook (v)	tham a-hanj, tham gap kao

cool	yen
cooperate	ruam meu
copy (photos/tapes)	at
copy/counterfeit	plawm
copyright	lik-ka-sit
coral	pa-ga-rang
corpse	sop
correct (v)	gae, gae kai
correct/correctly	thook
corrupt	kaw-rup-chan
count (v)	nap
country	pra-thet
countryside	ban nawk,
	chon-na-bot
coup d'etat	gan pa-tee-wat
court, go to court	keun san
cover (v)	pit, kloom
crash (into each other)	chon gan
crazy	ba
crazy and silly	ba-ba-baw-baw
credit (money)	ngeuhn phawn
cremate (a corpse)	phao sop
criminal	nak layng
criticize (say bad things)	tee
criticize/critique	wee-jan
cross/go across	kam
crowded/many people	kon mak, ae-at
crowded/tightly-packed	naen
cry	rawng hai

cry out	rawng
culture	wat-tha-na-tham
cure/convalesce	rak-saj
curve/curved	kong
customer	look ka
customs/traditions	pra-phay-nee
cut	tat
cut down trees	tat mai
cut your hair	tat phomj
cute	na rak

D

dam	keuan
dance	ten
dangerous	an-ta-rai
dare	gla
dark, colors	gae
dark, no light	meut
dead	tai laeo, siaj chee-wit
deaf	hooj nuak
debt	nee-sinj
decide	tat-sinj-jai
decimal point	joot
decorate	taeng
deep	leuk
deep/profound	leuk-seung
definitely	nae-nawn
delicious	a-roi

democratic	pra-cha-thip-pa-tai
demolish	thoop thing
deny	pa-tee-sayt
department (gov't)	nuay-ngan, grom, gawng
depends on	keun gap, laeo tae
deposit (when renting)	mat-jam
depressed/unhappy	gloom-jai
desert ("sea of sand")	tha-lay sai
design (n)	baep
design (v)	awk baep
design (on cloth/etc)	lai
destroy	tham-lai
details	rai-la-iat
develop	phat-tha-na
develop film	lang fim
developed	phat-tha-na laeo
developed/prosperous	ja-reuhn
dictator	pha-det-gan
dictionary	pot-ja-na-noo-grom (or "dictionary")
die (v)	tai, siaj chee-wit
different	mai meuanj
different from each other	mai meuanj gan, tang gan
difficult	yak
dig (v)	koot
direct/directly	trong
direction, compass	thit

direction/way	thang
dirty	mai sa-at, sok-ga-prok
disagree	mai hen duay
disappear	hai
disappointed	phit wang
distribute/give out	jaek
distribute/sell	jam-nai
dive	dam nam
divide up/share	baeng gan
divorce	ya
divorced (from each other)	yaek gan, ya gan
do/make	tham
doctorate	prin-ya ayk
document	ayk-ga-san
doll	took-ga-ta
donate	baw-ree-jak
dormitory	haw phak
down/go down	long
dozen	lo
draft into the army	gayn tha-han
dragon	mung-gawn
drama	la-kawn
draw	wat
draw a picture	wat roop
dream	fun
dress/get dressed	sai seua-pha
drink	gin, deum
drink liquor	gin lao
drive	kap

drown	jom-nam
drum	glawng
drunk/high	mao
dry	haeng
dry, for places	laeng, haeng-laeng
dust	foon
duty/responsibility	na-thee
dye (v)	yawm

E

each..	tae la..
each person	tae la kon
each other	gan (after verb)
earrings	toom hooj
earth (planet)	lok
earthquake	phaen din waij
east	ta-wan awk
easy/easily	ngai
easy/no problem	sa-bai
easy-going	jai-yen
eat	gin, than,
	rap-pra-than
	(three words, informal
	to formal)
economy	sayt-tha-git
education	gan seuk-saj
efficiency	pra-sit-thee-phap
elect	leuak ("choose")
election	gan leuak-tang

electricity	fai fa
elementary school	pra-thom﹆ seuk-sa﹆
embarrassed	ai
embrace/hug	gawt
emotion/mood	a-rom
end	sin, plai, thai
enemy	sat-troo
energy	gam-lang
engine	kreuang yon
enough	phaw
enter/go in	kao
entertain (guests)	rap-rawng
entrust (something)	fak
envelope	sawng jot-mai﹆
environment	sing-waet-lawm
envy/envious	eet-cha﹆
equal (to each other)	thao-gan
equipment	oop-pa-gawn
erase	lop
especially	doy cha-phaw
ethnic group	cheua chat
even if/although	theung﹆, mae wa
event/incident	hayt-gan
ever, have ever	keuy
every	thook, thook-thook
every kind/everything	thook yang
everybody	thook kon
evidence	lak-than﹆
examination, take an	sawp

83

examine/check	truat
example	tua yang
example, give an	yok tua yang
except	nawk-jak
excited	teun-ten
excrement	kee
exercise (v - physical)	awk gam-lang gai
exhaust (vehicle)	kwan rot
exhausted	phlia
expand	ka-yai
expect that	kat wa, ga wa
expenses	ka chai-jai
expensive	phaeng
experience (n)	pra-sop-gan
experience (v)	pra-sop
expert (person)	phoo chio-chan
expertly/well	geng
expired	mot a-yoo
explain	a-thee-bai
explode/burst	ra-beuht
expose to	tak
extend	taw
extinguish (fire/light)	dap
extravagant	foom-feuay
eyeglasses	waen ta

F

fade (colors)	seej tok
fail an exam	sawp tok

fair/festival	ngan
fair/just	yoot-tee-tham
faithful (in love)	jai-dio
fake	plawm
fall down/drop	tok
fall over	lom
famous	dang, mee cheu
fan	phat-lom
farm (garden)	suan
farm (plantation)	rai
farm (rice fields)	na
fashion	fae-chun
fast	reo, reo-reo
fat (adj)	uan
fat (n)	kai-mun
feel	roo-seuk
fence	rua
fertilizer	pui
festival	ngan, thayt-sa-gan
field (farm)	na, thoong na
field (sports/landing)	sa-nam
fight	toi, tee
fight with each other	toi gan, tee gan
fight (an army)	rop, soo-rop
fight/have problem with (a person)	mee reuang gap..
fill (a tooth)	oot
film	fim
finally	nai thee-soot

find	phóp, jeuh
find, can't find	haj mãi jeuh
fine (for an infraction)	pràp
fine/well	sà-bai dee
finish	tham hãi sèt
finished	sèt laeo
fire/electricity	fai
first, before something else	gawn
first, in a progression	(classifier) raek̂
first/at first	tawn raek̂
first class	chán nèung
fix	sawm̀
flag (of the country)	thŏng (chât)
flashlight	fai chaij
flat (for land)	râp
flat (for objects)	baen
flat tire	yang baen
flavor	rót, rót chât
flirt (with)	jeep
float	loi
float down (as on a raft)	lawng̀
floating market	tà-lat nam
flood	nam thuam
flour	paeng̀
flower	dawk-mai
fly (v)	bin
follow	tam
food	a-hanj

for/for the sake of	pheua
for/to give to	hai, samj-rap
for/to use for	chai
force/compel	bang-kap
foreign	tang pra-thet
forest	pa
forget	leum
forgive	hai a-phai
form (to fill out)	fawm
formal/official	thang-gan
fragile/easily broken	taek ngai
frame (picture frame)	grawp
free, have freedom	eet-sa-ra
free, no charge	"free"
free, not busy	wang
free time	way-la wang
freedom	sayj-ree-phap
fresh/uncooked	sot
fresh water	nam jeut
friend	pheuan
friend, to be friends	kop gan
friendly	jai-dee, pen gan ayng
friendship	mit-tra-phap
frightened/afraid	glua
frightened/startled	tok-jai
frightening	na glua
frying pan/wok	gra-tha
full, from eating	im
full, things	tem

fun	sa-nook
funeral	ngan sop
funny	ta-lok
fussy	joo-jee
future	a-na-kot

G

garbage	ka-ya
garden	suanj
gasoline	nam-mun
generation	roon
generous	mee nam-jai
genuine	thae
get/acquire	dai
get/receive	dai, dai rap
get dressed	sai seua-pha
get lost	longj thang
get married	taeng-ngan
get off/get out (vehicle)	long
get on/get in (vehicle)	keun
get ready	triam tua
get up	look keun
ghost	phee
gift	kawngj-kwanj
ginseng	somj
girlfriend	faen
give	hai
give back/return	keun
glass, drinking	gaeo

glass, window	gra-jòk
glasses	waen ta
glue	gao
go	pai
go across	kam
go back	glàp
go down/descend	long
go down/reduce	lót
go home	glàp ban
go in/enter	kaò
go out/emerge	awk
go out for fun	pai thio
go shopping	pai seu kawng
go to a movie	pai doo nang
go to school/be a student	rian nang-seu
go to see/visit	pai ha, yiam
go to see a doctor	pai ha maw
go to see a friend	pai ha pheuan
go to sleep	nawn
goal/objective	joot-moong-mai
God	Phra-jao
godfather	Ja pliaw
gold	thawng
gold color	see thawng
gone, disappeared	hai
gone, left already	pai laeo
gone, used up	mòt
good	dee

goods	sinj-ka
gossip (bad things)	nin-tha
government, local	thayt-sa-ban
government, national	rat-tha-ban
grade/level	chan
graduate	rian jop
grammar	wai-ya-gawn
grass	ya
gray	seej thao
green	seej kioj
group, music	wong don-tree
group, of people	gloom
grow, for people	to keun
grow, for plants	keun
grown up	to
guarantee (n)	pra-gan
guarantee (v)	rap-pra-gan
guard/watch over	fao
guess	dao, thai
guest	kaek
guilty (for infraction)	phit
guitar	gee-ta
gulf/bay	ao
gum, chewing	mak fa-rang
gun	peun

H

half	kreung (classifier)
half, one-half	kreung neung

hammer	$\overline{\text{kawn}}$
handsome	law
handwriting	lai meu
hang	kwaenj
hang, by the neck	kwaenj kaw
happen	geuht, geuht keun
happy, general feeling	mee kwam-sook
happy/glad	dee-jai
hard (opp. soft)	kaengj
hard/difficult	$\overline{\text{yak}}$
hard/heavily	nak
hard-working	ka-yanj
harvest rice	gio $\overline{\text{kao}}$
hate	gliat
have	mee
have ever (done something)	keuy
have to/should	tawng
health	sook-ka-phap
healthy	sook-ka-phap dee
hear	$\overline{\text{dai}}$ yin
hear news	$\overline{\text{dai}}$ yin kao
heart/mind (ก้าวหน้า)	jai
heaven	sa-wanj
heavy	nak
height/altitude	kwam-soongj
hell	na-rok
help	chuay, chuay leuaj
here	thee-nee

91

heroin	hay-ro-een
herself	kao ayng
hide	sawn
high/tall	soong,
high school	mat-tha-yom seuk-sa,
himself	kao ayng
hire	jang
history	pra-wat-tee-sat
hit/bump into	chon
hit/fight	toi
hit/punch/box	chok
hit/strike	tee
hold	jap, theu,
hole	roo
holiday	wan yoot
holy	sak-sit
home	ban
homeless child	dek ray-rawn
homesick	kit theung, ban
homework	gan-ban
homosexual, female	thawm
homosexual, male	gay, ga-theuy (second is derogatory)
honest	seu-sat
honor/prestige	giat
hook (for fishing)	bet
hope that..	wang, wa..
horoscope, consult	doo duang
hot (temperature)	rawn

hot/spicy	phet
house	ban
human being	ma-noot
humid	op-ao
hungry	hiu) kao

I

idea	kwam-kit
if	tha
illegal	phit got-mai)
important	sam)-kan
impossible	pen pai mai dai
impressed (by)	pra-thap-jai
improve/make better	prap-proong
improved/better	dee keun
in advance	luang na
in case	pheua
in order to	pheua
in style/up-to-date	than sa-mai)
incense	thoop
inch	niu
include	ruam
income	rai dai
increase	pheuhm
independence	eet-sa-ra-phap
indifferent	cheuy)-cheuy)
industry	oot-sa-ha)-gam
inflation	ngeuhn feuh

information	kaw-moon
inner tube	yang nai
innocent	baw-ree-soot
insect	ma-laeng
insecticide	ya ka ma-laeng
inspect	truat
instead (of)	thaen, thaen thee
insurance, health	pra-gan sook-ka-phap
insurance, life	pra-gan chee-wit
intelligent	cha-lat
interested (in)	sonj-jai
interesting	na sonj-jai
interview	samj-phat
introduce	nae-nam
invade	book
involved	gio kawng
involves	gio (gap)
iron (v - clothes)	reet
island	gaw

J

jail, in jail	tit kook
jealous (in love)	heungj
jealous/envious	eet-chaj
joke (v)	phoot len

K

keep	ao wai

keep doing/continuously	reuay-reuay
key	goon-jae
kick	tay
kill	ka
kilogram	gee-lo-gram, lo
kilometer	gee-lo-met
kind/nice	jai-dee
kind/type	yang, baep, cha-nit, pra-phayt (last two are more formal)
king	nai luang, ga-sayt
kiss (Thai style)	hawm (also means "nice-smelling")
kiss (western style)	joop
kite	wao
know, general	roo
know, polite	sap
know a person/place	roo-jak
knowledge	kwam-roo

L

lack	kat
ladder	bun-dai
lake	tha-lay sap
land (piece of land)	thee-din
land measuring unit	rai (1600 sq. meters)
lane/side street	soi
language	pha-sa
lantern	ta-giang

last/endure	thon
last/final	soot-thai
last name	nam sa-goon
late (at night)	deuk
late/not on time	cha, mai than
laugh	hua ɹ-raw
law	got-mai ɹ
lazy	kee-giat
leader	phoo nam
learn	rian, rian roo
leave	awk pai
left (side)	sai
left/leftover	leua ɹ
leftovers (food)	a-han ɹ leua ɹ
lend ("let borrow")	hai yeum
let/allow	hai, a-noo-yat
let's..	..gan theuh
letter	jot-mai ɹ
letter of the alphabet	tua
level (n)	ra-dap
library	hawng sa-moot
lie/tell a lie	go-hok
lie down	nawn
life	chee-wit
lift, something large	yok
lift, something small	yip
light, electric	fai
light, in weight	bao
light, to describe colors	awn

like/like to	chawp
like/similar/alike	klai-klai gan
like/similar to..	klai-klai..
like/the same as..	meuanɟ..
like more/prefer	chawp mak gwa
like that/in that way	yang-ngan
like the most	chawp mak thee-soot
like this/in this way	yang-ngee
limit/limited	jam-gat
listen (to)	fang
liter	leet
literature	wan-na-ka-dee
litter (v)	thing ka-ya
little (size)	lek
little/a little (amount)	noi, nit noi
live at	yoo
live with	yoo gap
local/native	pheun meuang
lock (n)	goon-jae
lock (v)	lawk
lonely	ngaoɟ
long, a long time	nan
long, in length	yao
look (at)	doo
look for	haɟ
look down on/insult	doo thook
look like	doo meuanɟ
loose	luamɟ
lose/cause to be lost	tham haiɟ

lose face	siaj nâ
lose weight	lot kwam ûan
lose your way	lŏngj thang
lost/gone (thing/person)	haij
lottery	lawt-ta-reê, huayj
lotus flower	dawk bua
loud/loudly	dang
love (n)	kwam rák
love (v)	rák
low	tàm
luck	chôk
lucky/good luck	chôk dee

M

machine	kreuang
machinery	kreuang jak
mad, angry	gròt, mo-hoj
mad, crazy	bâ
magazine	nang-seuj,
	nìt-ta-ya-sanj
magic, black magic	saij-ya-sàt
make/cause to happen	thâm hâi
make/do	thâm
make a mistake	phìt, thâm phìt
make up your face	taeng nâ
man	phoô-chai
manage	jàt-gan
manners/behavior	nee-saij

manners/etiquette	ma-ra-yat
many/a lot	mak, yeuh
map	phaenj thee
marijuana	gan-cha
market	ta-lat
marriage license	tha-bian somj-rot
married	taeng-ngan laeo
marry	taeng-ngan
massage	nuat
master's degree	prin-ya tho
matches	mai keet fai
mathematics	ka-nit-sat
maybe	bang-thee
meaning	kwam-maij
means, it means	maij-kwam wa..
measure	wat
medicine	ya
meet	phop, jeuh
meet/have a meeting	pra-choom
member	sa-ma-chik
menstrual period	pra-jam deuan
message	kaw-kwam
meter	met
method	wi-thee
middle	glang
might	at ja (verb)
might/maybe	bang-thee
military base	gawng thap bok
mind/heart (figurative)	jai

mindfulness (Buddhism)	sa-ma-thee
minister, government	rat-tha-mon-tree
ministry, government	gra-suang
minus	lop
miss, a person or place	kit theung,
mistake/mistaken	phit
mistress	mia noi
misunderstand	kao-jai phit
mix	pha-som, ruam
modern	sa-mai, mai
Mon (ethnic group)	Mawn
money/silver	ngeuhn
mood, good mood	a-rom dee
mood/emotion	a-rom
moon	phra jan
moonlight	saeng, jan
more/add on	pheuhm
more/again	eeg
mortar, to pound food	krok
mosquito	yoong
mosquito net	moong
mosquito repellant	ya gan yoong
most/mostly	suan mak
most/the most	mak thee soot
mountain	phoo-kao,
move (residence)	yai
move/shift position	leuan
movie	nang, phap-pha-yon
movie star	da-ra nang,

mud	klon
murder	kat-ta-gam
music	don-tree
music/song(s)	phlayng
musical instrument	kreuang don-tree
must (strong meaning)	jam-tawng
must/have to	tawng
mute person	kon bai
myself, for men	phom ayng
myself, for women	chan ayng

N

nail	ta-poo
name	cheu
name, last	nam sa-goon
narrow	kaep
national	haeng chat
national park	oot-tha-yan haeng chat
nationality	san-chat
nature/natural	tham-ma-chat
navy	gawng thap reua
neat/neatly	riap-roi
need (v)	tawng-gan
needle	kem
negotiate	jay-ra-ja
neighbor	pheuan ban
net, fishing (round)	hae
never/have never	mai keuy
new	mai

news	kao
newspaper	nang-seuj phim
next/the following	taw pai
nice (person)	jai-dee
nice-smelling	hawmj
nickname	cheu len
nightmare	funj rai
nobody	mai mee krai, mai mee kon
noise	siangj
noisy	siangj dang
normal	tham-ma-da, pok-ga-tee
normally/as usual	tam pok-ga-tee
north	neuaj
northeast	ta-wan awk chiangj neuaj
northwest	ta-wan tok chiangj neuaj
not many	mai mak
not very..	mai koi..
not yet	yang, yang mai..
notebook	sa-moot
nothing	mai mee a-rai
number, seat/room	beuh
number/numeral	maij lek
nursery school	a-noo-ban

O

obey	cheua fang
object/thing	kawng
occupation	a-cheep
ocean (large)	ma-ha sa-moot
ocean/sea	tha-lay
odor/scent	glin
official/royal	luang
oil	nam-mun
oil, engine	nam-mun kreuang
OK/it's agreed	tok-long
old, living things	gae
old, objects	gao
old-fashioned	bo-ran
on time	than, than way-la
one-way	thang dio
only (a small amount)	kae.., ..thao-nan
only (one kind)	..yang-dio, tae.. ("but")
open	peuht
opinion	kwam kit-hen
opium	fin
opportunity	o-gat
or	reu
orchid	dawk gluay mai
order (v)	sang
ordinary/regular	tham-ma-da
organization	ong-gan
original (of a document)	ton cha-bap
original/first	deuhm

other/some other	(classifier) eun
our/ours	kawng) rao
over/finished	jop laeo
owner (of)	jao kawng)

P

pack (bags)	gep kawng)
paddle	phai
paid (already)	jai laeo
paint (v)	tha see)
painting (n)	roop-wat, phap-wat
pair	koo
palace	phra-thee-nang
pants/trousers	gang-gayng
paper	gra-dat
papers/documents	ayk-ga-san)
parade/procession	hae
park, a vehicle	jawt
park/garden	suan)
parliament	rat-tha-sa-pha
part (of something)	suan
part/region	phak
participate	mee suan ruam
parts (for a vehicle)	a-lai
party	ngan pa-tee, gin liang, ngan liang
party, political	phak gan meuang
pass, a car	saeng
pass, a test	sawp dai, sawp phan

pass through/pass by	phan
passenger	phoo doy-sanɟ
past	a-deet
path	thang deuhn
patient, of a doctor	kon kai, phoo puay
patient/easy-going	jai yen
pave/paved	lat yang
pavilion	saɟ-la
pawn	jam-nam
pay (v)	jai
pay attention to	ao jai sai
pay for/treat	liang
pay taxes	siaɟ pha-seeɟ
peace	sunɟ-tee-phap
peaceful	sa-ngop
peak	yawt
peek at	aep doo
peel (v)	pawk
pen	pak-ga
pencil	din-sawɟ
people/common people	chao ban
people/person	kon
people/the people	pra-cha-chon
percent	peuh-sen
perfect	somɟ-boon baep
perfume	nam-hawmɟ
period (at end of sentence)	joot
period (in history)	sa-maiɟ
period/duration	chuang

permanent	pra-jam, thaj-wawn
permit (n)	bai a-noo-yat
permit/allow	hai, a-noo-yat
person/people	kon
personal	suan tua
personality	book-ka-lik
photocopier	kreuang thai ayk-ga-san
photograph (n)	roop, roop thai
pick up, a person	pai rap
pick up, large object	yok
pick up, small object	yip
pickled	dawng
picture, drawing	phap wat
picture, photograph	roop
piece	chin
pill	met
pimp	maeng da
pink	seej chom-phoo
pipe, for water/gas	thaw
pirate	jon sa-lat
pity	songj-sanj
place	thcc, sa-thanj-thee
place, this place	thee-nee
plan (n)	phaenj
plan/plan to (v)	wang phaenj
planet/star	dao
plant (n)	ton-mai
plant (v)	plook

play (v)	len
play/drama	la-kawn
plow	thaij
pocket	gra-paoj
point (at)	chee
point/pointed	laemj
point/score	ka-naen
poison (n)	ya phit
poisonous	mee phit
polite	soo-phap
political party	phak gan meuang
politics	gan meuang
polluted	siaj, pen phit
poor	jon
popular	nee-yom
population	phon-la-meuang,
	pra-cha-gawn
powder	paeng
power/authority	am-nat, it-thee-phon
power/strength	gam-lang, raeng
practice	sawm
pray	a-theet-thanj
prefer	chawp mak gwa
pregnant	mee thawng
prejudiced (against..)	mee a-ka-tee (gap..)
prepare/get ready	triam, triam tua
present/gift (n)	kawngj-kwanj
present/propose (v)	sa-neuhj
present/the present time	pat-joo-ban

preserve/conserve	rak-saj, a-noo-rak
president	pra-tha-na thi-baw-dee
pretty	ngam
previous	deuhm
price	ra-ka
primary school	pra-thomj
prime minister	na-yok rat-tha-mon-tree
prince	jao chai
princess	jao yingj
prison, in prison	tit kook
prisoner	nak thot
private (company)	ayk-ga-chon
private/personal	suan tua
probably	kong ja (verb)
problem(s)	pan-haj
produce/manufacture	pha-lit
profession	a-cheep
program	rai-gan
prohibit	ham
project	krong-gan
promise	sunj-ya
promote/foster	song-seuhmj
propose/offer	sa-neuhj
protect/defend	pawng-gan
proud/pleased	phoom-jai
prove	phee-soot
public (adj)	saj-tha-ra-na
pull (on)	deung

punish	tham thot
pure/innocent	baw-ree-soot
purple	seej muang
purse/bag	gra-paoj
push	phlak
put away/keep	gep wai
put down	wang
put in/put on	sai
put on clothes	sai seua-pha
put on make-up	taeng na
put out (fire/lights)	dap
put together/combine	ruam

Q

quality	koon-na-phap
quantity/amount	jam-nuan
queen	ra-cha-nee
question (n)	kam thamj
quick/quickly	reo, reo-reo
quiet	ngiap
quit, a job	la awk
quit/stop	leuhk

R

race/compete	kaeng, kaeng-kunj
radio	wit-tha-yoo
rafting	lawng phae
raise (an animal)	liang

rape	kōm keuŋ
rare/hard to find	haj yak
rate	àt-tra
rather, I'd rather..	..dee gwa
raw	dip
razor	meet gon
razor blade	bai meet
read	an
read (as an activity)	an nàng-seuj
read it to me	an hai fang
ready/finished	sèt laeo
ready/prepared	riap-roi, phrawm
real	thae
reason	hàyt-phonj
receipt	bai sèt
receive	dai, dai ràp
recommend	nae-nam
red	seej daeng
reduce	lòt
reduce weight	lòt kwam uan
refugee	phoo òp-pha-yop
register (v)	jòt tha-bian
regular	tham-ma-da
relative/relation (people)	yat
release	plòi
remember	jam
rent (v)	chaò
rent/charter (rent a vehicle entirely)	maoj

rent to someone/"for rent"	hai chao
repair/fix	sawm
reply (v)	tawp
report (v)	rai-ngan
representative	phoo-thaen
require	tawng-gan
research (v)	wee-jai
resemble	doo meuang
reserve	jawng
respect/believe in	nap-theu
respect/show respect	kao-rop
respond	tawp
responsible (for)	rap-phit-chawp
rest (v)	phak-phawn
rest, the rest/leftover	thee leuang
restroom	hawng nam
results	phon
return (something)	keun
return, come back	glap ma
return, go back	glap pai
revolution	gan pa-tee-wat
rhythm/beat	jang-wa
rice	kao
rich	ruay
rich person	sayt-thee
ride	kee
right (side)	kwa
right/correct	thook, thook-tawng

rights, have rights	mee sit
ripe/cooked until done	sook
river	mae-nam
road/street	tha-non
road/way/route	thang
rob/steal	plon, ka-moy
rock	hin
rocket	ja-ruat
rope	cheuak
rose	dawk goo-lap
rotate	moon
rotten	nao
round/circular	glom
royal	luang
rubber	yang
rubber tree	ton yang
ruins ("old city")	meuang gao
ruler, for measuring	mai ban-that
rumor	kao-leu
run	wing
run away	nee
run into/crash into	chon
run into/meet	jeuh

S

safe	plawt-phai
said that	phoot wa
sailboat	reua bai
sailor	tha-han reua

salary	ngeuhn deuan
salty/salted	kem
same/equal	thao-gan
same as.. (referring to characteristics)	meuanj..
same as each other	meuanj-gan
same/one and the same	dio-gan
same person	kon dio-gan
same place	thee dio-gan
sand	sai
sanitary napkin	pha a-na-mai
sarong	sa-rong
satellite	dao thiam
satisfied	phaw-jai
save	gep wai
save money	gep ngeuhn
saw (tool)	leuay
say	phoot
say that..	phoot wa..
schedule/timetable	ta-rang way-la
scholarship	thoon
school	rong-rian
science	wit-tha-ya-sat
scissors	gun-grai
scold	da
score (n)	ka-naen
screwdriver	kaij kuang
sea	tha-lay
seat	thee-nang

second (in time)	wee na-thee
second (number two)	thee sawng
see	hen
see a movie	doo nang
seed	met
seems like	doo meuan
selfish/self-centered	hen gae tua
sell	kai
send	song
sentence (in language)	pra-yok
separate (v)	yaek
separately	tang hak
serious (good conno- tation)	jing-jang
serious/tense	kriat
service	baw-ree-gan
set (n)	choot
set up	tang
sew	yep
sew, make clothes	tat seua
sex, have sex	len sek
sex/gender	phet
shade	rom
shadow	ngao
shake hands	jap meu
shampoo	ya sa phom
share/divide up	baeng
share/use together	chai ruam gan
sharp	kom

shave	gon nuat
shell/shellfish	hoi
ship (n)	reua
shoot	ying
shoot a gun	ying peun
shop (n)	ran
shop/shopping	seu kawng
short, in height	tia
short, in length	sun
should	na ja, kuan ja (both followed by verb)
shout	rawng
show (n)	gan sa-daeng, cho
show (v)	sa-daeng
shrink	hot ("hote")
shy	ai, kee ai
Siam	Sa-yam
side	kang
sight/eyesight	sai ta
sign (signboard)	pai
sign language	pha-sa meu
sign your name	sen cheu
signal	sun-yan
similar to each other	klai-klai gan
sin	bap
sincere	jing-jai
sing	rawng phlayng
single/only one	(classifier) dio
single/unmarried	sot

sink (v)	jom-nam
sit	nang
size, clothing	sai
size/extent	ka-nat
skill	kwam sa-mat
skin (n)	phiuj
skin/hide	nangj
sky	fa
slang	sa-laeng
slave	that
sleep/lie down	nawn
sleep/is sleeping	lap, nawn lap
sleep, can't sleep	nawn mai lap
sleepy	nguang nawn
slice	hun
slip/slippery	leun
slow/slowly	cha, cha-cha
small	lek
smell/odor	glin
smell/sniff	dom
smells bad	menj
smells good	hawmj
smile	yim
smoke (n)	kwan
smoke from a fire	kwan fai
smoke cigarettes	soop boo-ree
smooth	riap
smuggle	lap lawp konj
snack (n)	ka-nomj

snack (v)	gin len
sneeze	jam
snore	gron
so/therefore	leuy, gaw leuy
so that/in order to	pheua
soap	sa-boo
society	sangɟ-kom
soft (for sounds)	bao
soft (to the touch)	nim
software	sawf-wae
soil	din
solve	gae kaiɟ
some	bang (followed by classifier)
some people	bang kon
some/somewhat	bang
song(s)	phlayng
sorry/excuse me	kawɟ-thot
sorry/unhappy	siaɟ-jai
sound	siangɟ
sour	prio
south	tai
southeast	ta-wan awk chiangɟ tai
southwest	ta-wan tok chiangɟ tai
space/outer space	a-wa-gat
spark plug	huaɟ thian
speak	phoot
speak/converse	kui
speaker/loudspeaker	lum-phong

special	phee-set
speed	kwam-reo
spell (v)	sa-got
spend money	chai ngeuhn
spirit	win-yan
spit/saliva	nam-lai
spit out	thuij
spoiled, food	siaj
sponsor (v)	sa-nap sa-noonj
spray	cheet
squeeze	beep
staff/staffmember	pha-nak-ngan
stage	way-thee
stand	yeun
stand up/get up	look keun
star	dao
stare (at)	jawng
start	reuhm
starve	ot, ot kao
state, as in United States	rat
state/condition	sa-phap
station	sa-thaj-nee
statue	roop pun
status	thaj-na
stay	phak
stay at home	yoo ban
stay overnight	kang keun
steal	ka-moy
stick (wood)	mai

stick to	tit
sticky	nioj
still/yet	yang
stingy	kee nioj
stolen/disappeared	haij
stone/rock	hinj
stop	yoot
stop/park a vehicle	jawt
story, a story to tell	reuang lao
story/fable	nee-than
story/floor	chan
straight	trong
strict/rigid/austere	kem nguat
strange	plaek
stream	huay
street/road	tha-nonj
street/side street/lane	soi
stretch	yeut
string/rope	cheuak
strong	kaengj-raeng
stubborn/disobedient	deu
study	rian
stupid	ngo
style/kind	baep
subject, in school	wee-cha
subject/topic	reuang
substitute/replace	thaen
suburb(s)	chan meuang
succeed/finish	samj-ret

succeed/get results	dai phon
suck	doot
suck/keep in the mouth	om
suck/pump	soop
suffer	thaw-ra-man
suicide, commit	ka tua tai
suitcase	gra-pao
sun	phra a-thit
sunbathe	ab-daet
sunburn	phiu mai
sunflower	than ta-wan
sunrise	phra a-thit keun
sunset	phra a-thit tok
suntan lotion	keem gan daet
superstition	chok lang
supervise	koom
suppose that	som-moot wa
sure/surely	nae-jai, nae nawn
surprised/shocked	tok-jai
surrender	yawm phae
suspect/wonder	song-sai
suspect that	song-sai wa
swamp	beung, nawng (first is larger)
sweat (n)	ngeua
sweat (v)	ngeua awk
sweep	gwat
sweet	wan
swim	wai-nam

swimming pool	sa wai-nam
sword	dap
sympathize	henj-jai
symptom	a-gan
system	ra-bop

T

tail	hangj
take (something away)	ao pai
take/want	ao
take a bath	ab-nam
take a picture	thai roop
take a trip	pai thio
take a walk	deuhn len
take advantage of	ao priap
take care of	doo-lae
take medicine	gin ya
take off clothes	thawt seua-pha
take off shoes	thawt rawng-thao
talented	mee phawn sa-wanj
talk/converse	kui
talk/say/speak	phoot
talk about.. (a subject)	phoot reuang..
tall	soongj
tape, cassette	thayp
tape recorder/radio	wit-tha-yoo thayp
taste (in styles)	rot-sa-nee-yom
taste/flavor	rot ("rote"), rot chat
taste/try	chim

tattoo (n)	roi sak
tattoo (v)	sak
tax (n)	pha-see
tax, pay tax	sia pha-see
teach	sawn
tear down	thoop thing
tease (v)	law len
tease flirtatiously	saeo
technical school	thek-nik
teenager	wai-roon
television	tho-ra-that
tell	bawk
tell that/told that	bawk wa
temperature	oon-ha-phoom
temporary/temporarily	chua-krao
term/semester	theuhm
terrible/awful	yae
test, take a test	sawp
that (as in "I think that")	wa
that (as in "that one")	(classifier) nan
that (as in "the shirt that")	thee
that (a thing)	nan
their/theirs	kawng kao
then (two actions)	laeo gaw
then/at that time	tawn-nan
there/over there	thee-nan
there/way over there	thee-noon
there is/there are	mee
there isn't/there aren't	mai mee

therefore/so	leuy, gaw leuy
thick (in width)	naj
thick/concentrated	kon
thief	jon, ka-moy
thin, for objects	bang
thin, for people	phawmj
thing/things/objects	kawngj
think	kit
think that	kit wa
thirsty	hiuj nam
this (as in "this shirt")	nee
this (a thing)	nee
this is..	nee keu...
this kind	yang-ngee, baep nee
this one	un nee
this person	kon nee
this place	thee-nee
this way/like this	yang-ngee
this way/this route	thang nee
thread	dai
through/finished	set laeo
throw	yon
throw away	thing
ticket	tuaj
tickles/it tickles	jak-ga-jee
tie (v)	phook, mut
tight-fitting	kap
tightly	sa-nit
time	way-la

tire, for vehicle	yang, yang rot
tire, flat	yang baen
tired (mentally and physically)	neuay
tired/sore	meuay
to/in order to	pheua
together	duay-gan
together/put together	ruam
toilet	hawng nam
told (already)	bawk laeo
told me that	bawk wa
ton	tun
tone, in speaking Thai	ra-dap siang
too (as in "too hot")	pai, geuhn pai
too/also	duay
too (together)	duay-gan
too (the same)	meuan-gan
tool	kreuang meu
tooth	fun
tooth, false	fun plawm
toothbrush	praeng see fun
toothpaste	ya see fun
toothpick	mai jim fun
torn	kat
touch	jap, don
tough (meat)	nio
tourism	gan thawng-thio
toward	taw
town	meuang

toy	kawngງ len
trade/commerce	gan ka
trade/swap	laek
trademark	kreuang maiງ
tradition/culture	wat-tha-na-tham
tradition/custom	pra-phay-nee
traditional/old-style	sa-maiງ gao
traditional/original	deuhm
traffic	ja-ra-jawn
train (v)	feuk
transfer	on ("own")
translate	plae
trash	ka-ya
travel (v)	deuhn-thang
treat/pay for	liang
tree	ton mai
tribe	phao
trophy	thuay
trouble, be in	deuat-rawn
trouble/problem, have	mee pan-haງ
true	jing
trust (v)	wai-jai
try/make an effort	pha-ya-yam
try/test out	lawng
tube	lawt
turn, a corner	lio
turn/revolve	moonງ
turn off ("close")	pit
turn on ("open")	peuht

twice	sawngɟ krang
twins (children)	look faet
type (v)	phim deet
type/kind	yang, baep, cha-nit, pra-phayt
typewriter	kreuang phim deet

U

ugly	na gliat
umbrella	rom
understand	kao-jai
undress	thawt seua-pha
unemployed	tok ngan
unfriendly	mai pen mit
unhappy	siaɟ-jai
unhappy (lost something)	siaɟ-daɟ
uniform	choot, kreuang baep
United Nations	Sa-ha Pra-cha-chat
universal/international	saɟ-gon (used for western music, boxing)
universe	jak-gra-wan
university	ma-haɟ-wit-tha-ya-laɟ
unless	nawk-jak
unlucky	suay, chok mai dee
unmarried	sot
unripe/not fully cooked	mai sook
up	keun
upset	mai sa-bai jai

use	chai
used/second hand	chai laeo
used to, in the past	keuy
used to/accustomed to	chin
used up	mot
useful	mee pra-yot
usually/as usual	pok-ga-tee
usually/mostly	suan mak
usually/regularly	tham-ma-da

V

vacation	phak rawn
valuable	mee ka
value	ka
various	tang-tang
vehicle	rot ("rote")
very	mak
video player	kreuang len wee-dee-o
video tape	wee-dee-o
view	wiu
village	moo-ban
violin	gontr
visa	wee-sa
visit (a place)	pai thio
visit (go to see a person)	pai haj, yiam
vitamin	wit-ta-min
vocabulary	kam sap
volcano	phoo-kaoj fai
volunteer (v)	a-saj, a-saj-sa-mak

vote (for)	leuak
vowel	sa-ra

W

wage	ka jang
wait/wait for	koi, raw
wake someone up	plook
wake up	teun, teun nawn
walk	deuhn
wall (city/garden)	gam-phaeng
want/take	ao
want/would like/need	tawng-gan
want to	yak, tawng-gan
war	song-kram
warehouse	go-dang
warm	oon
warn	teuan
wash	lang
wash clothes	sak seua-pha
wash dishes	lang jan
wash your face	lang na
wash your hair	sa phom
waste	sia
waste money	sia ngeuhn
waste time	sia way-la
watch (n)	na-lee-ga
watch TV	doo tho-ra-that
water	nam
waterfall	nam-tok

wave (ocean)	kleun
way/method	wi-thee
way/route	thang
weapon	a-woot
wear/put on	sai
wedding	ngan taeng-ngan
weigh	chang
weight	nam-nak
welcome	yin dee tawn rap
well (for water)	baw
well/expertly	geng
well/fine	sa-bai dee
well-mannered	riap-roi
west/western	ta-wan tok
wet	piak
wheat	kao saj-lee
wheel	law
whether (or not)	mai wa
who ("the person who")	thee
whisper	gra-sip
whistle (v)	phiuj pak
white	seej kaoj
wide	gwang
will/would	ja
wipe	chet
wire	luat
wire, electrical	saij fai
woman	phoo-yingj
wonder if	songj-saij wa

wonderful	jaeoj, yiam
wood	mai
word	kam
work (v)	tham-ngan
work/job	ngan
world	lok ("loke")
worry/be concerned	pen huang
worth it	koom, koom ka
would be better	..dee gwa
would like (to)	tawng-gan
write	kianj
wrong/wrongly	phit, mai thook

X

xylophone	ra-nat

Y

yellow	seej leuangj
yet/still	yang
young	awn
yourself	koon ayng

Z

zero	soonj
zoo	suanj sat

THAI PHRASEBOOK

Phrases are marked (f) if they have the women's pronoun for "I" (*chan*) and the polite word *ka*. They're marked (m) if they have "I" for men (*phom*) and the polite word *krup*.

Greetings

Hello. (said by a woman)	Sa-wat-dee ka.
Hello. (said by a man)	Sa-wat-dee krup.
Where are you going?	Pai naiŋ?
I'm going out.	Pai thio.
Where have you been?	Pai naiŋ ma?
I've been to the market.	Pai ta-lat.
Are you well?	Sa-bai dee reu plao?
Yes, I'm well.	Sa-bai dee.
Thank you. (f)	Kawp-koon ka.
Thank you. (m)	Kawp-koon krup.
It's nothing./That's OK.	Mai pen rai.
excuse me (f)	kawŋ-thot ka
excuse me (m)	kawŋ-thot krup

good luck	chok dee
goodbye (informal)	Pai gawn, na.
goodbye (polite)	Sa-wat-dee ka/krup.
See you again.	Phop gan mai.
goodbye/farewell	la gawn
You're invited.	Cheuhn.
Please sit down.	Cheuhn nang.
Please come in.	Cheuhn kao ma.

General Phrases

Isn't that right?	Chai mai?
Yes./That's right.	Chai.
No./That's not right.	Mai chai.
maybe	bang-thee
I'm not sure.	Mai nae-jai.
I don't know.	Mai roo.
certainly/for sure	nae-nawn
really/truly	jing-jing
Is that true?	Jing reu plao?
Oh?/Really?	Reuhj?
no problem	mai mee pan-haj
anything/whatever	a-rai gaw dai
anywhere/wherever	thee-naij gaw dai
any time/whenever	meua-rai gaw dai
Help!	Chuay duay!
calm down	jai yen-yen

wait a minute	dioɟ, dioɟ-dioɟ
be careful	ra-wang
hurry up	reep noi, reo-reo noi
It's up to you.	Laeo tae koon.
Do whatever you like.	Tam sa-bai.
I'm indifferent.	cheuyɟ-cheuyɟ
I can't do it (physically).	mai waiɟ
just right	phaw dee
adequate/alright	phaw chai dai
the best/the greatest	yiam
that's it/that's all	kae nee

Making Friends

What's your name (m)?	Koon cheu a-rai, krup?
My name is Daeng (f)	Chan cheu Daeng.
Where are you from?	Koon ma jak naiɟ?
I'm from Chiang Mai. (m)	Phomɟ ma jak Chiang Mai.
Have you eaten yet?	Gin kao reu yang?
Yes, I've eaten already.	Gin laeo.
No, not yet.	Yang.
Where are you going?	Koon ja pai naiɟ?
I'm going home. (f)	Chan ja glap ban.
Where's your house?	Ban yoo thee-naiɟ?
It's in Bang Na.	Yoo Bang Na.

Personal Information

address	thee-yoo
May I have your address?	Kawj thee-yoo noi.
Where were you born?	Koon geuht thee-naij?
I was born in Chiang Mai. (f)	Chan geuht thee Chiang Mai.
How old are you?	Koon a-yoo thao-rai?
I'm 20. (m)	Phomj a-yoo yee-sip.
Are you married?/Do you have a boy/girlfriend?	Koon mee faen reu yang?
Yes, I do. ("already")	Mee laeo.
No. ("not yet")	Yang.

Passport/Cards

credit card	bat kray-dit
May I use this card?	Chai bat nee dai mai?
driver's license	bai kap kee
I.D. card	bat pra-jam tua
passport	phat-sa-pawt
visa	wee-sa
extend	taw
I have to extend my visa. (f)	Chan tawng taw wee-sa.
immigration office	gawng truat kon kao meuang
business card	nam-bat
May I have your card?	Kawj nam-bat noi.

Languages

Thai	pha-saj Thai
English	pha-saj Ang-grit
French	pha-saj Fa-rang-set
German	pha-saj Yeuh-ra-mun
central Thai (language)	pha-saj glang
Can you speak English?	Koon phoot pha-saj Ang-grit dai mai?
Yes./No.	Dai./Mai dai.
Can you speak Thai?	Koon phoot pha-saj Thai dai mai?
Just a little.	Dai nit noi.
I can't speak Thai. (m)	Phomj phoot pha-saj Thai mai dai.
She/He can speak Thai.	Kao phoot pha-saj Thai dai.
Is there someone who can speak English?	Mee krai phoot pha-saj Ang-grit dai bang?
teach	sawnj
Can you teach me Thai? (m)	Koon sawnj pha-saj Thai hai phomj dai mai?
read	an
What does this say? (reading something)	Nee an wa a-rai?
It says "welcome".	An wa "yin dee tawn rap".

135

Understanding/Saying

Do you understand?	Koon kao-jai mai?
Yes, I understand.	Kao-jai.
I don't understand	Mai kao-jai.
What?	A-rai, na?
What did you say?	Koon phoot wa a-rai, na?
Please speak slowly.	Phoot cha-cha noi.
Please say that again.	Chuay phoot eeg krang neung, dai mai?
What does "pla" mean?	"Pla" mai-kwam wa a-rai?
It means "fish".	Mai-kwam wa "fish".
What's it called in Thai?	Pha-sa Thai riak wa a-rai?
It's called a "broom".	Riak wa "mai gwat".

Question Words

What?

Some of the following questions have *bang* (with a falling tone) at the end. It's included when the question might have more than one answer, to make it sound less demanding.

what	a-rai
What's this?	Nee (keu) a-rai?
This is a map.	Nee keu phaen-thee.
What are you doing?	Tham a-rai?

I'm studying Thai. (f)	Chan rian pha-saj Thai.
What are you doing today?	Wan-nee koon ja tham a-rai bang?
I'm going to see Wat Pho.	Phomj ja pai thio Wat Pho.
What shall we do?	Tham a-rai dee?
Let's go to a movie.	Pai doo nangj gan theuh.
What did you buy?	Koon seu a-rai bang?
I bought a book. (m)	Phomj seu nang-seuj.
I didn't buy anything.	Mai dai seu a-rai.
What do you think?	Koon kit wa a-rai?
I think he's coming today.	Kit wa kao ja ma wan-nee.
What did she say?	Kao phoot wa a-rai?
She said she isn't coming.	Kao phoot wa kao mai ma.
What happened?	Geuht a-rai keun?
Two cars crashed.	Rot chon gan.
What's wrong?	Pen a-rai?
I have a headache. (f)	Chan puat huaj.
Nothing.	Mai mee a-rai.

Which?

For "which" put *nai* after the classifier of the object you're referring to.

which	(classifier) naij

general classifier for objects	ùn
Which one?	Un naiŋ?
Which one do you want?	Ao ùn naiŋ?
I want this one.	Ao ùn nee.
classifier for buildings	lang̣
Which building?	Lang̣ naiŋ?
Which building do you stay in?	Koon yoo lang̣ naiŋ?
In that building.	Yoo lang̣ nan.

What kind?

kind, smaller units	yang, cha-nìt
type/style, larger units	baep, pra-phayt
(second in each is more formal)	
what kind?	yang naiŋ?
what type?/what style?	baep naiŋ?
What kind do you want?	Ao yang naiŋ?
(choosing kinds of food, etc)	
I want this kind.	Ao yang nee.
What type of food do you like?	Koon chawp a-hanŋ baep naiŋ?
I like spicy food.	Chawp a-hanŋ phet-phet.
What style of suit do you want?	Ao choot baep naiŋ?
I want this style.	Ao baep nee.
I want this style of shirt.	Ao seua baep nee

Who?

who	krai
Who did you come with?	Koon ma gap krai?
I came with a friend. (f)	Chan ma gap pheuan.
Who are you going with?	Koon ja pai gap krai?
I'm going with Lek. (m)	Phom ja pai gap Lek.
I'm going alone. (f)	Chan ja pai kon dio.
which person	kon nai
Which person is named Daeng?	Kon nai cheu Daeng?
This person./That person.	Kon nee./Kon nan.
Did anyone come to see me? (f)	Mee krai ma haj chan mai?
Two people came to see you.	Mee sawng kon ma haj koon.
nobody	mai mee krai
Nobody came.	Mai mee krai ma.

Where?

where	thee-nai, nai
Where's your house?	Ban yoo thee-nai?
It's here.	Yoo thee-nee.
It's over there.	Yoo thee-nan.
It's way over there.	Yoo thee-noon.
Where are you going?	Koon ja pai nai?
I'm going to the hotel. (f)	Chan ja pai rong-raem.
I'm not going anywhere.	Mai pai nai.

Where did you go last night?	Meua-keun-nee koon pai naij?
I went to the disco.	Pai thio thek.
I didn't go anywhere.	Mai dai pai naij.
Where is Dam?	Dam yoo thee-naij?
Where did Daeng go?	Daeng pai naij?
He/She went to the bank.	Kao pai pai tha-na-kan.
I don't know where she went.	Chan mai roo wa kao pai naij.
Where's the suitcase?	Gra-paoj yoo thee-naij?
It's in the room.	Yoo nai hawng.
Where do they sell batteries?	Mee than fai-chaij kaij thee-naij?
They sell them over there.	Mee kaij yoo thee-noon.

How?

how (informal/formal)	yang-ngai/yang-rai
How is this hotel?	Rong-raem nee pen yang-ngai?
It's good.	Dee.
How do you feel?	Koon pen yang-ngai?
Fine.	Sa-bai dee.
How are you going to Pattaya?	Koon ja pai Phat-tha-ya yang-ngai?
I'm going by air-conditioned bus.	Pai rot-thua./Nang rot-thua pai.

Why?

Put *tham-mai* at the end of affirmative questions ("Why are you../Why did you..?") and at the beginning of negative questions ("Why aren't you../Why didn't you..?").

why	tham-mai
Why are you going to Had Yai?	Koon ja pai Had Yai tham-mai?
I'm going for fun.	Pai thio.
Why aren't you going to Songkla?	Tham-mai koon mai pai Songj-klaj?
because	phraw, phraw wa
Because I don't have time.	Phraw wa mai mee way-la.
Why didn't you call me? (m)	Tham-mai koon mai dai tho ma haj phomj?
I forgot your phone number. (f)	Chan leum beuh tho-ra-sap.

Numbers

Cardinal Numbers

Numbers in Thai are simple. If you know one to ten you can make almost any number.

1, 2, 3	neung, sawngj, samj
4, 5	see, ha
6, 7, 8	hok, jet, paet
9, 10	gao, sip

For numbers in the teens put the unit number after ten. The exception is 11 which is *sip-et*, not *sip-neung.*

11, 12	sip-et, sip-sawngɟ
13, 14	sip-samɟ, sip-see
15, 16	sip-ha, sip-hok
17, 18	sip-jet, sip-paet
19	sip-gao

Do the same for numbers in the twenties.

20, 21	yee-sip, yee-sip et
22	yee-sip sawngɟ
23	yee-sip samɟ
24	yee-sip see
25	yee-sip ha

30, 40, 50, and other two-digit numbers have the unit number before *sip.*

30, 40	samɟ-sip, see-sip
50, 60	ha-sip, hok-sip
70, 80	jet-sip, paet-sip
90	gao-sip

Add the unit number.

35	samɟ-sip ha
48	see-sip paet
64	hok-sip see
75	jet-sip ha

hundred	r̄oi
thousand	phận
ten thousand	meun
hundred thousand	saenɟ
million	lan̄
billion	phận lan̄
500	h̄a r̄oi
750	jėt r̄oi h̄a-sip
1,500	nẹung phận h̄a r̄oi
shortened form	phận h̄a
2,000	sawngɟ phận
3,000	samɟ phận
10,000	nẹung meun
20,000	sawngɟ meun
35,000	samɟ meun h̄a phận
shortened form	samɟ meun h̄a
400,000	see saenɟ
5,000,000	h̄a lan̄

Ordinal Numbers/Dates

Put *thee* (with a falling tone) before cardinal numbers to make ordinal numbers, which are used in dates and for things in series.

first/number one	theē neung
second/number two	theē sawngɟ
the second person	kon theē sawngɟ
the third house	langɟ theē samɟ

143

the fourth chapter	bot thee see
date	wan thee
the 1st	wan thee neung
the first of August	wan thee neung deuan
	Singj-haj
what date?	wan thee thao-rai?
What date are you	Koon ja ma wan thee
coming?	thao-rai?
I'm coming on the 10th.	Ma wan thee sip.

"The first" when referring to things in a series is *raek*, not *thee neung*.

the first day (ie. of a trip)	wan raek
the first time	krang raek

How much?

how much	thao-rai
How much money do you	Koon mee ngeuhn
have?	thao-rai?
I have five thousand	Phomj mee ngeuhn ha
baht. (m)	phan baht.
How much money did you	Koon hai ngeuhn kao
give him?	thao-rai?
I gave him a thousand	Chan hai kao neung
baht. (f)	phan baht.

144

How many?

Use classifiers to refer to numbers of objects. The classifier for people is *kon*, which in this case is the same as the noun "person/people". "How many people" is *gee kon* and "two people" is *sawng kon*.

how many	<u>gee</u> (classifier)
person/classifier for people	kon
how many people?	<u>gee</u> kon
How many people are going?	Pai <u>gee</u> kon?
Four people are going.	Pai <u>see</u> kon.
day/classifier for days	wan
how many days	<u>gee</u> wan
How many days are you going for?	Pai <u>gee</u> wan?
I'm going for three days.	Pai <u>sam</u>ɟ wan.

What time?

The system used for telling time in Thai is complicated. The day is divided into four 6-hour periods and each has its own word for "hour" or "o'clock". Officially a 24-hour clock is used with the word *na-lee-ga* for "o'clock". Some times can be expressed in two or more ways

6 am	<u>hok</u> mong <u>chao</u>
7 am	<u>jet</u> mong <u>chao</u>
8 am	<u>paet</u> mong <u>chao</u>,
	<u>sawng</u>ɟ mong <u>chao</u>

9 am	gaŏ mong chao,
	samɟ mong chao
10 am	sip mong chao,
	see mong chao
11 am	sip-et mong chao,
	ha mong chao
noon	thiang
1 pm	bai mong
2 pm	bai sawngɟ
3 pm	bai samɟ
4 pm	bai see
5 pm	ha mong yen
6 pm	hok mong yen
7 pm	neung thoom
8 pm	sawngɟ thoom
9 pm	samɟ thoom
10 pm	see thoom
11 pm	ha thoom
midnight	thiang keun
1 am	tee neung
2 am	tee sawngɟ
3 am	tee samɟ
4 am	tee see
5 am	tee ha

Add *kreung* for "half past". For minutes say the number followed by *na-thee*. *Tawn*, translated as "at", can be included before any time phrase.

What time is it?	<u>Gee</u> mong?
	<u>Gee</u> mong laeo?
It's 10:30. (am)	<u>Sip</u> mong kreung.
What time are you going home?	Koon ja glap ban gee mong?
I'm going home at 5:15. (pm)(f)	Chan ja glap ban tawn ha mong sip-ha na-thee.

When?
Days/Weeks

Monday	wan Jan
Tuesday	wan Ang-kan
Wednesday	wan Phoot
Thursday	wan Pha-reu-hat
Friday	wan Sook
Saturday	wan Sao⌡
Sunday	wan A-thit
weekend	sao⌡ a-thit
weekday	wan tham-ma-da
this Monday	wan Jan nee
next Monday	wan Jan na
last Monday	wan Jan thee laeo

Ja is usually included before verbs for sentences in the future, but it's optional and can be omitted. Without *ja* the same sentence could be interpreted as past, present, or future with the meaning understood by the context it's spoken in.

when	meua-rai
what day	wan naij
When are you going to Lopburi?	Koon ja pai Lop-boo-ree meua-rai?
I'm going to Lopburi on Friday. (m)	Phomj ja pai Lop-boo-ree wan Sook.
What day did she go to Khon Kaen?	Kao pai Kawnj Gaen wan naij?
She went last Sunday.	Kao pai wan A-thit thee laeo.

today	wan-nee
yesterday	meua-wan-nee
tomorrow	phroong-nee
minute	na-thee
hour	chua-mong
day	wan
week	a-thit
month	deuan
year	pee
this week	a-thit nee
next month	deuan na
last week	a-thit thee laeo
last year	pee thee laeo
a moment ago	meua-gee-nee
in three days	eeg samj wan

in two weeks	eeg sawng̯ a-thit
five days ago	ha wan thee laeo
four years ago	see pee thee laeo
When is your friend coming?	Pheuan ja ma meua-rai?
My friend's coming next week.	Pheuan ja ma a-thit na.
When did you come?	Koon ma meua-rai?
I came two days ago. (m)	Phom̯ ma sawng̯ wan thee laeo.
When is the bus leaving?	Rot ja awk meua-rai?
In ten minutes it's leaving.	Eeg sip na-thee ja awk.

How Long?

Questions with "how long" are usually phrased as "How many days/weeks?", etc. *Laeo* is included for "already". You can also ask ""Have you...long?" with the person's response giving the amount of time he/she has been doing the activity.

How many days have you been here?	Koon ma gee wan laeo?
I've been here for five days.	Yoo ha wan laeo.
Have you...long?	Koon...nan reu yang?
Have you been in Thailand long?	Koon yoo meuang Thai nan reu yang?

Yes./a long time	Nan.
No./not a long time	Maï nan.
I've been in Thailand for one month. (f)	Chan yoo meuang Thai neung deuan laeo.
for two more days	eeg sawng/ wan
for a long time more	eeg nan
I'll be here for one more week. (m)	Phom/ ja yoo eeg neung a-thit.
all day	thang wan
all night	thang keun
I couldn't sleep all night. (f)	Chan nawn maï lap thang keun.
always/all the time	ta-lawt, sa-meuh/
I want to stay here always. (m)	Phom/ yak yoo thee-nee ta-lawt.

Other Time Phrases

now	tawn-nee
right now	dio/-nee
Ann's in Australia now.	Tawn-nee Ann yoo Aws-tray-lia.
We're going right now.	Rao ja pai dio/-nee leuy.
morning	tawn chao
this morning	tawn chao nee
early afternoon (1-4 pm)	tawn bai
this afternoon (early)	tawn bai nee

late afternoon (5-7 pm)	tawn yen
this afternoon (late)	tawn yen nee
last night	meua-keun-nee
I went to Wat Phra Keo this morning (m).	Tawn chao nee phom pai Wat Phra Gaeo.
tonight	keun-nee
I'm going to a party tonight.	Keun-nee phom ja pai ngan pa-tee.
after	lang-jak
after that	lang-jak nan
I'm going shopping this afternoon. (f)	Tawn bai nee chan ja pai seu kawng.
After that I'm going to the embassy.	Lang-jak nan chan ja pai sa-than-thoot.
before	gawn
I went to Sukothai before coming here. (m)	Phom pai Soo-ko-thai gawn ma thee-nee.
before/in the past	meua-gawn
I was a teacher before. (f)	Meua-gawn chan pen kroo.
since	tang-tae
I've been here since Friday. (m)	Phom you thee-nee tang-tae wan Sook.
until	theung, jon gra-thang
from..to..	tang-tae..theung..
soon	reo-reo nee
just	pheung
She just came.	Kao pheung ma.

when ("when I went")	tawn, meua
When I went to Chiang Mai I visited Doi Suthep. (f)	Tawn chan pai Chiang Mai, chan pai thio Doi Soo-thayp.

Months/Years

Formally the names of months have a final syllable, either *kom*, *phan*, or *yon*, which isn't included here.

January	deuan Mok-ga-ra
February	deuan Goom-pha
March	deuan Mee-na
April	deuan May-saj
May	deuan Phreut-sa-pha
June	deuan Mee-thoo-na
July	deuan Ga-ra-ga-da
August	deuan Singj-haj
September	deuan Gan-ya
October	deuan Too-la
November	deuan Phreut-sa-ji-ga
December	deuan Than-wa
what month	deuan naij
What month are you coming back?	Koon ja glap ma deuan naij?
I'm coming back in April. (f)	Chan ja glap ma deuan May-saj.

Thailand uses Buddhist Era years, which are 543 years before Christian Era years.

A.D. (Christian Era)	krit-ta-sak-ga-rat
abbreviation	kaw saw)
B.E. (Buddhist Era)	phoot-tha-sak-ga-rat
abbreviation	phaw saw)
what year?	pee naij
What year were you born?	Koon geuht pee naij?
I was born in 1980 (2518).	Phom) geuht pee
("one-eight")	neung-paet.

Appointments

meet	phop, jeuh
When are you meeting her?	Koon ja phop kao meua-rai?
I'm meeting her at noon. (m)	Phom) ja phop kao tawn thiang.
appointment	nat
I have an appointment with him tomorrow. (f)	Chan mee nat gap kao phroong-nee.
free	wang)
busy/not free	mai wang
Are you free tonight?	Keun-nee wang mai?
I'm not free tonight. (m)	Keun-nee phom) mai wang.
When should we meet?	Phop gan meua-rai dee?

Is tomorrow morning OK?	Phroong-nee chao dee mai?
Yes.	Dee.
invite	chuan
He invited me to a party. (f)	Kao chuan chan pai gin liang.
Do you want to go?	Koon ja pai mai?

How many times?/How often?

There are three words for "time" or "occasion". The first is the most common.

time/occasion	krang, thee, hon
how many times?	gee krang?
two times	sawng krang
one time	neung krang, krang dio
many times	lai krang
How many times have you come to Thailand?	Koon ma pra-thet Thai gee krang laeo?
I've been here twice.	Ma sawng krang laeo.

Questions with "how often" are usually phrased as "How many times a week?", "How many times a month?", etc.

each/per	la
how many times a week?	a-thit la gee krang
How often do you study Thai? (How many times a week?)	Koon rian pha-sa Thai a-thit la gee krang?

I study Thai three times a week. (f)	Chan rian pha-saj Thai a-thit la samj krang.
every two months	thook sawngj deuan
I go to Malaysia every three months. (m)	Phomj pai Ma-lay-sia thook samj deuan.
every day	thook wan
I eat Thai food every day.	Chan gin a-hanj Thai thook wan.
all the time	ta-lawt way-la
sometimes	bang thee, bang krang
often	boi
He comes here often.	Kao ma thee-nee boi.

Telephone

Thais usually use polite language on the phone, especially when talking with someone they don't know. *Koon* is put before names and *ka* or *krup* is added to every sentence.

telephone	tho-ra-sap
mobile phone	meu theuj
telephone number	beuh tho-ra-sap
telephone line	saij
May I speak to Lek. (f)	Kawj saij koon Lek, ka.
This is Lek. (m)	Nee Lek, krup.
Just a moment. (f)	Sak kroo, ka.
Goodbye. (m)	Sa-wat-dee krup.
May I leave a message?	Fak kaw-kwam wai dai mai?

155

Please tell him/her that Noi called.	Chuay bawk kao wa koon Noi tho ma haj.
Please tell him/her to call me. (f)	Chuay bawk kao hai tho ma haj chan.
call a place	tho pai
I'd like to call Vietnam. (f)	Kawj tho pai Wiet Nam dai mai, ka?
call here	tho ma
Someone called you.	Mee kon tho ma haj koon.
extension	taw
I'd like extension 12. (m)	Taw sawngj-ha krup.
fax	faek, tho-ra-sanj
May I send a fax? (m)	Kawj song faek dai mai, krup?

Shopping

Ka or *krup* should be included with *thao-rai* ("how much"), as a single word can sound rude.

How much?	Thao-rai, ka/krup?
How much is this?	Un nee thao-rai?
How much is it for two?	Sawngj un thao-rai?
Will you take 100 baht?	Roi baht dai mai?
Can you reduce the price?	Lot hai noi, dai mai?
How much is it altogether?	Thang-mot thao-rai?
change from a purchase	ngeuhn thawn

THAI PHRASEBOOK

I haven't received my change.	Yang maï daï ngeuhn thawn.
May I have a receipt?	KawɈ bai-set noi.
May I exchange this? (f)	KawɈ plian un nee daï maï, ka?

Kuat, "bottle", is the classifier used to refer to things in bottles.

Do you have drinking water?	Mee nam-plao maï?
How much is a bottle?	Kuat la thaò-rai?
A bottle is ten baht.	Kuat la sip baht.

Tua, meaning "body", is the classifier for clothing. "This shirt" is literally "shirt, this body" — *seua tua nee*.

| How much is this shirt? | Seuaʼ tua nee thaò-rai? |
| This shirt is 200 baht. | Seuaʼ tua nee sawngɈ roi baht. |

Un in these sentences is the general classifier, used to refer to any object.

Do you want this one? (f)	Ao un nee maï, kaɈ?
Yes. (m)	Ao, krup.
No. (f)	Maï ao, ka.
How many do you want?	Ao gee un?
I want one. (three ways to say)	Ao neung un./Ao un neung/Ao un dio.
I want two.	Ao sawngɈ un.

157

Clothing

bathing suit, men's	gang-gayng wai nam
bathing suit, women's	choot wai-nam
belt	kem̩ kut
hat	muak
jacket/coat	seua gan nao̩
jeans	gang-gayng yeen
purse	gra-pao̩
sarong	sa-rong
shirt	seua
T-shirt	seua yeut
shoes	rawng-thao
shorts	gang-gayng ka̩ sun
skirt	gra-prong
socks	thoong̩ thao
suit	choot
sunglasses	waen gan daet
sweater	seua gan nao̩
underwear	gang-gayng nai

classifier for pants/shirts	tua
This shirt is nice.	Seua tua nee suay̩.
May I try it on? (f)	Lawng sai dai mai, ka?
Does it fit?	Sai dai mai?
It fits./I can wear it.	Sai dai.
It doesn't fit./I can't wear it.	Sai mai dai.
classifier for shoes/socks	koo ("pair")
Do you like this pair?	Chawp koo nee mai?

Made of

What's this made of?	Nee tham duay a-rai?
It's made of...	Tham duay...
brass	thawng leuang
copper	thawng daeng
cotton	pha fai
gold	thawng
iron	lek
ivory	nga, nga chang
jade	yok
leather	nang
metal	lo-ha
plastic	plas-tik
silk	pha mai
silver	ngeuhn
steel	lek gla
teak	mai sak
things that are fake	kawng plawm
things that are genuine	kawng thae
This is a fake.	Nee pen kawng plawm.

Jewelry

jewelry	kreuang pra-dap
gemstone	phloi
diamond	phet
emerald	maw-ra-got
ruby	thup-thim

sapphire	nin
blue sapphire	phai-lin
classifier for gemstones	met
How much is this gem-stone?	Met nee thao-rai?
ring	waenj
classifier for rings	wong
How much is this ring?	Wong nee thao-rai?
necklace	soi, soi kaw
bracelet	soi kaw meu, gam-lai
classifier for strands	sen
How much is this necklace?	Sen nee thao-rai?

Food

breakfast	a-hanj chao
lunch	a-hanj glang wan
dinner	a-hanj yen
food	a-hanj
seafood	a-hanj tha-lay
dessert/snack	kawngj wanj, ka-nomj
vegetarian food	a-hanj jay
order food	sang a-hanj
May I have..?	Kawj...
May I have a menu?	Kawj may-noo duay.
May I have a menu in English?	Kawj may-noo pha-saj Ang-grit.

to go (in a bag)	sai thoong)
I'd like iced coffee to go.	Kaw) ga-fae yen sai thoong).
put	sai
without meat	mai sai neua
without MSG	mai sai phong) choo rot
without sugar	mai sai nam-tan
without milk	mai sai nom
not hot/spicy	mai phet
without chili pepper	mai sai phrik
cooked until done/ripe	sook
not fully cooked/unripe	mai sook
raw	dip
I'm a vegetarian. (m)	Phom) gin jay.
I didn't order this.	Un nee mai dai sang
Waiter!/Waitress!	Nawng!
Check please. (cheap restaurant)	Gep-tang duay).
Check please (expensive restaurant)	Chek-bin duay).
Keep the change.	Mai tawng thawn.

Order food by numbers of plates, bowls, etc.

bottle	kuat
large bottle	kuat yai
small bottle	kuat lek
bowl, large	cham
bowl, small	thuay)

cup	thuay
glass	gaeo
plate	jan
chopsticks	ta-giap
fork	sawm
knife	meet
spoon	chawn
straw	lawt
I'd like one plate of fried rice with chicken.	KawɈ kao-phat gai neung jan.
I'd like one bottle of drinking water.	KawɈ nam-plao neung kuat.
I'd like two glasses of water.	KawɈ nam-plao sawngɈ gaeo.
How much is a bottle of beer?	Bia kuat la thao-rai?

drinks	kreuang deum
beer	bia
draft beer	bia sot
coffee, hot	ga-fae rawn
coffee, iced	ga-fae yen
ice	nam kaengɈ
lemonade	nam ma-nao
liquor	lao
milk	nom
orange drink	nam som
orange juice (fresh)	nam som kun
banana smoothie	gluay pun

pineapple smoothie	sap-pa-rot pun
rice wine	lao kaoj
soda water	nam so-da
tea	nam-cha
tea, Chinese	nam-cha jeen
water, drinking	nam plao
whisky/liquor	lao
wine	lao wai
condiments/garnishes	kreuang proong
basil	bai hoj-ra-pha
spicy basil	ga-phrao
coconut milk	nam ga-thee
coriander leaf	phak chee
curry paste/chili sauce	nam phrik
curry powder	phongj ga-ree
fermented fish	pla-ra, pla-daek
fish sauce	nam pla
galanga (ginger-like root)	ka
garlic	gra-thiam
ginger	kingj
honey	nam pheung
MSG	phongj choo rot
onions	hawmj yai
oyster sauce	nam-mun hoij
pepper, chili	phrik
pepper, small/very hot	phrik kee nooj
pepper, black	phrik thai
salt	gleua

soy sauce	see iu
sugar	nam-tan
vegetables	phak
bamboo shoots	naw-mai
beans (string/green)	thua fuk yao
cabbage	ga-lum
cashew nuts	met ma-muang
cauliflower	ga-lum dawk
corn	kao-phot
baby corn	kao-phot awn
cucumber	taeng gwa
eggplant (small)	ma-keuaj
eggplant (long)	ma-keuaj yao
lettuce	phak-gat
morning glory	phak boong
green vegetable, large leaves	phak ka-na
mushrooms	het
pea pods	thua lun tao
peanuts	thua
potatoes	mun fa-rang
squash	fuk
tofu	tao-hoo
tomatoes	ma-keuaj-thet
meat	neua
beef	neua, neua wua
chicken	gai

duck	pet
eggs	kai
fish	pla
frog	gop
innards	kreuang nai
liver	tap
meatballs	look chin
pork	mooj
pickled pork	naemj
pork bologna	mooj yaw
wild boar	mooj pa
sausage	sai grawk
water buffalo meat	neua kwai
fish	pla
catfish	pla dook
crab	poo
shellfish	hoij
shrimp	goong
squid	pla meuk
white rice	kao
steamed white rice	kao plao
sticky rice	kao nioj
rice soup	kao tom
brown rice	kao glawng
noodles	guay-tioj
large white noodles	sen yai
small white noodles	sen lek

yellow noodles	ba-mee
bread	ka-nomj pang
toast	ka-nomj pang ping
butter	neuy
cheese	neuy kaengj
jam	yaem
fried eggs	kai dao
omelet	kai jio
stuffed omelet	kai yat-sai
ham	mooj haem
french fries	mun fa-rang thawt
stir-fried	phat
sweet and sour	prio-wanj
sweet and sour shrimp	goong phat prio-wanj
chicken with ginger	gai phat kingj
beef with spicy basil	neua phat ga-phrao
catfish with curry paste	pla dook phat phet
fried morning glory	phat phak boong
fried mixed vegetables	phat phak ruam mit
vegetable salad	sa-lat phak
spicy papaya salad	som-tam
vegetarian	jay
vegetarian "phak kana"	phak ka-na jay
fried/deep-fried	thawt
fried chicken	gai thawt
fried pork with garlic	mooj thawt gra-thiam
tempura	choop paeng thawt

curry/soup	gaeng
hot red curry with beef	gaeng phet neua
green curry with chicken	gaeng kioj-wanj gai
boiled/soup	tom
spicy soup with shrimp	tom yam goong
mildly seasoned soup	tom jeut
spicy salad	yam
spicy salad with squid	yam pla meuk
minced meat	lap
spicy minced chicken	lap gai
barbecued	yang
barbecued chicken	gai yang
steamed	neung
steamed crab	poo neung
roasted	op
roasted chicken	gai op
fruit	phonj-la-mai
banana	gluay
coconut	ma-phrao
durian	thoo-rian
grapes	a-ngoon
guava	fa-rang
jackfruit	ka-noonj
lime	ma-nao
longan	lum-yai
lychee	lin-jee
mango	ma-muang

mangosteen	máng-kóot
papaya	má-lá-gaw
pineapple	sáp-pa-rót
rambutan	ngaw
sugar cane	ói
tamarind	má-kamɟ
tangerine	sómˋ
watermelon	taeng mo

How much is a kilo? (f)	Lo thaó-rai, ka?
A kilo is 40 baht.	Lo lá see-sip baht.
I'd like one kilo.	Ao gée-lo neung.
I'd like two kilos.	Ao sawngɟ gée-lo.
How much is this piece of fruit?	Look nee thaó-rai?
I'd like this piece.	Ao look nee.

People

adult	phoó yai
baby (up to two years)	dèk awn
baby (two to five years)	dèk lék
baby, have a	awk look, klawt look
child/children	dèk
boy	dèk phoó-chai
girl	dèk phoó-yingɟ
man	phoó-chai
young man	noom
woman	phoó-yingɟ

young woman	sao̯

Family

family	krawp-krua
mother	mae̯
father	phaw̯
parents	phaw-mae̯
older sister	phee-sao̯
younger sister	nawng-sao̯
older brother	phee-chai
younger brother	nawng-chai
brothers and sisters	phee-nawng
wife	faen, mia, phan-ra-ya
	(usually *phá-lá-ya*)
husband	faen, sa̯-mee
children (of your own)	look̯
daughter	look-sao̯
son	look-chai
grandmother, maternal	yai
grandmother, paternal	ya̯
grandfather, maternal	ta
grandfather, paternal	poo̯
aunt, older sister of mother or father	pa̯
uncle, older brother of mother or father	loong
aunt/uncle, younger on mother's side	na

169

aunt/uncle, younger on father's side	ah
cousin	look-phee-look-nawng
grandchild/niece/nephew	lanɲ
relative	yat
classifier for people	kon
How many children do you have?	Koon mee look gee kon?
I have two children. (f)	Chan mee look sawngɲ kon.
I don't have any children.	Mai mee look.
This is my older brother.	Kon nee pen phee-chai.
He's visiting Thailand.	Kao ma thio pra-thet Thai.
He came with his wife.	Kao ma gap faen.

Countries

Kon is put before the name of countries for people of different nationalities. *Chao* (meaning "inhabitant of") is also used in some phrases. *Meuang* and *pra-thet* both mean "country", and *meuang* also means "city". The word *farang* is used generally for westerners. It shouldn't be thought of as derogatory.

Thai (person)	kon Thai
American (person)	kon A-may-ree-ga
westerner	fa-rang

foreign country	tang pra-thet
foreigner	kon tang pra-thet
Asia	Ay-sia
Asian	chao Ay-sia
Europe	Yoo-rop
European person/people	chao Yoo-rop
Indian/Muslim person	kaek
hilltribe person	chao kaoɟ
Africa	A-free-ga
America	A-may-ree-ga, Sa-ha-rat
Australia	Aws-tray-lia
Bali	Ba-leeɟ
Burma/Myanmar	Pha-ma
Cambodia	Ka-menɟ,
	Gum-phoo-cha
Canada	Kae-na-da
China	meuang Jeen
England	pra-thet Ang-grit
France	Fa-rang-set
Germany	Yeuh-ra-mun
Hong Kong	Hawng Gong
India	In dia
Indonesia	In-do-nee-sia
Italy	It-ta-lee
Japan	Yee-poon
Korea	Gao-leeɟ
Laos	pra-thet Lao,
	meuang Lao

Malaysia	Ma-lay-sia
Middle East	Ta-wan awk glang
Philippines	Fee-lip-peen
Russia	Rat-sia
Saudi Arabia	Sa-oo
Singapore	Sing-ka-po
Switzerland	Sa-wit
Vietnam	Wiet Nam

Use the name of the country to make adjectives like "German" and "French".

Have you ever eaten Italian food?	Koon keuy gin a-han It-ta-lee mai?

Occupations

actor/actress	nak sa-daeng
airplane pilot	nak bin
ambassador	thoot
architect	sa-thaj-pa-nik
artist	chang wat roop
athlete	nak gee-la
barber	chang tat phom
businessman/woman	nak thoo-ra-git
construction worker	chang gaw sang
cook	kon krua
cook, female	mae krua
cook, male	phaw krua
dentist	maw fun

doctor	maw̌j
driver	kon kàp rót
electrician	chàng fai-fá
engineer	weet-sà-wá-gawn
farmer	chao na
fisherman	kon hǎj pla
fortune teller	maw̌j doo
guard/watchman	yam
government worker	kâ-rât-chá-gan
guide	gai
housewife	mae bân
laborer	gam-má-gawn
lawyer	thá-nai, thá-nai kwam
masseur/masseuse	maw̌j nûat
mechanic	chàng sawm̌ rót
model, female	nang baep
model, male	nai baep
musician	nák don-tree
nurse	phá-ya-ban,
	nang phá-ya-ban
police officer	tam-rùat
politician	nák gan meuang
professor	à jan
prostitute	sǒj-phay-nee,
	ga-lee (vulgar)
psychiatrist	jìt-tà-phaet
reporter	nák kao
scientist	nák wìt-thá-ya-sàt
secretary	lay-kǎj

seller, female	maē kā
seller, male	phāw kā
servant	kòn chāi
singer	nak rawng
soldier	thǎ-hanǰ
student	nak rian
teacher	kroo
tourist	nak thawng thiǒ
translator	lam, phoo phlae
boss (n)	huaǰ nā
manager	phoo jàt-gan
assistant	phoo chuay
employee	lookǰ jang
staff/staffmember	phà-nāk-ngan
company	baw-ree-sàt
factory	rong-ngan
office	awf-fìt

What work do you do?	Koon tham-ngan a-rai?
I'm a secretary. (f)	Chan pen lay-kaǰ.
Where do you work?	Koon tham-ngan thee-naiǰ?
I work in Lard Phrao. (m)	Phomǰ tham-ngan thee Lat Phrao.
Do you have a day off?	Mee wan yoot mai?
I'm off on Sunday.	Yoot wan A-thit.

Business

business	thoo-ra-git
business/company	baw-ree-sat
capital, for investment	thoon, ngeuhn thoon
invest	long thoon
They invested in this company.	Phuak kao long thoon nai baw-ree-sat nee.
stock/share	hoon
stock market	ta-lat hoon
The stock market is going up.	Ta-lat hoon keun.
The stock market is going down.	Ta-lat hoon long.
import	nam kao
goods	sinj-ka
This company imports goods from Japan.	Baw-ree-sat nee nam sinj-ka kao jak pra-thet Yee-poon.
export	song awk
This company exports rice.	Baw-ree-sat nee song awk kao.
wholesale	kaij song
retail	kaij pleek
profit	gam-rai
This company makes a good profit.	Baw-ree-sat nee dai gam-rai dee.
lose money in business	kat thoon
go bankrupt	lom-la-lai

Bank

bank	tha-na-kan
account	ban-chee
I'd like to open an account.	Kawɟ peuht ban-chee noi.
branch, of a bank/etc	saɟ-kaɟ
cash (money)	ngeuhn sot
bills	baeng
coins	rianɟ
dollar	dawn, dawn-la
cash a check	keuh ngeuhn
I'd like to cash a check.	Kawɟ keuh ngeuhn noi.
exchange money	laek
I'd like to exchange money.	Kawɟ laek ngeuhn noi.
change/small bills	baeng yoi
Do you have change? (small bills)	Mee baeng yoi mai?
deposit	fak
withdraw	beuhk, thawnɟ
I'd like to withdraw some money.	Kawɟ beuhk ngeuhn noi.
travelers check	chek deuhn-thang
ATM card	bat ATM
interest	dawk bia

Post Office

post office	prai-sà-nee
stamp	sà-taem
letter	jòt-maiʲ
package/parcel	phát-sà-dòo
Send this to America. (m)	Sòng ùn nee pai A-may-ree-ga krup.
register	long thá-bian
I'd like to register it.	Kawʲ long thá-bian duay.
Are there any letters for me? (f)	Mee jòt-maiʲ theungʲ chan mai?

Body

body	tua
abdomen/stomach	thawng
arm	kaenʲ
back	langʲ
beard	krao
blood	leuat
blood vessel	senʲ leuat
bone	grà-dòok
brain	sà-mawngʲ
breasts	nom
buttocks	gon
chest	òk
ear	hooʲ
eye	ta

177

face	nā
finger	niu
fingernail	lep meu
foot	thao
hair, on the body	koŋ
hair, on the head	phomŋ
hand	meu
head	huaɟ
heart	huaɟ-jai
kidney	tai
knee	huaɟ kao
leg	kaɟ
lips	rim feeɟ pak
liver	tap
lungs	pawt
moustache	nuat
mouth	pak
muscle	glam
nerves	pra-sat
nose	ja-mook
skin	phiuɟ
stomach	gra-phaw
throat/neck	kaw
tongue	lin
tooth	fun
waist	eo

Medical

Please call a doctor.	Chuay riak maw duay.
a doctor who can speak English	maw thee phoot pha-sa Ang-grit dai
I want to go to the hospital.	Chan yak pai rong-pha-ya-ban.
Please call an ambulance.	Chuay riak rot pha-ya-ban duay.
I'm not well. (f)	Chan mai sa-bai.
I'm ill. (f)	Chan puay.
I have a fever. (f)	Chan pen kai.
I have a cold. (f)	Chan pen wat.
I have a cough. (f)	Chan ai.
ache	puat
I have a headache. (m)	Phom puat hua.
I have a stomachache.	Phom puat thawng.
I have diarrhea. (f)	Chan thawng sia.
I have no strength.	Mai mee raeng.
abscess	fee
AIDS	rok ayt
allergic to..	phae
backache	puat lang
broken leg	ka hak
cancer	ma-reng
cut (finger/etc)	bat
dengue fever	kai leuat awk
disease/sickness	rok ("roke")

dizzy	wian hua
faint	pen lom
food poisoning	a-han pen phit
flu	kai wat yai
hurt/it hurts	jep
hurt/injured	bat jep
infected	ak-sayp
itches	kun
malaria	ma-la-ria
numb	cha
operate	pha tat
sore throat	jep kaw
swollen	buam
tetanus	bat-tha-yak
typhoid fever	thai-foi
unconscious	sa-lop, mot sa-tee
vomit	uak, a-jian
weak	awn ae
worms (intestinal)	pha-yat
wound	phlae
medicine	ya
traditional medicine	ya phaen bo-ran
get an injection	cheet ya
blood test/test blood	truat leuat
band-aid	plas-teuh
medicine to relieve..	ya gae..
Do you have cough medicine?	Mee ya gae ai mai?

Take this medicine.	Gin ya nee.
How many should I take?	Gin gee met?
Take two.	Gin sawngɟ met.
How many times a day?	Wan la gee krang?
Three times a day.	Wan la samɟ krang.

Places in Town

bank	tha-na-kan
barber shop	ran tat phomɟ
beauty shop	ran seuhmɟ suayɟ
bookstore	ran kaiɟ nang-seu
drugstore	ran kaiɟ ya
embassy	sa-thanɟ-thoot
fountain	nam phoo
gas station	pum nam-mun
hotel	rong-raem
market, produce	ta-lat sot
movie theater	rong-nangɟ
museum	phee-phit-tha-phan
park	suanɟ
police station	sa-thaɟ-nee tam-ruat
post office	prai-sa-nee
school	rong-rian
swimming pool	sa wai-nam
tailor	ran tat seua
restaurant	ran-a-hanɟ
shopping center	soonɟ gan-ka
intersection, 4-way	see yaek

intersection, 3-way	sam̄ɉ yaek
street/road	thà-nǒnɉ
side street	soi
expressway	thang duan
traffic circle	wong-wian
bridge	sà-phan
canal	klawng

Add *ka* (for women) and *krup* (for men) to be polite when asking strangers for directions.

Where's the hospital? (m)	Rong-phà-ya-ban yoo thee-naiɉ, krup?
It's over there.	Yoo thee-noon.
turn right	lio kwaɉ
turn left	lio sai
go straight	trong pai
Which side is it on?	Yoo kang naiɉ?
It's on the right.	Yoo kang kwaɉ.
It's on the left.	Yoo kang sai.
Which way should I go?	Pai thang naiɉ?
Go this way.	Pai thang nee.
What street is it on?	Yoo thà-nǒnɉ a-rai?
It's on Sukhumvit Rd.	Yoo thà-nǒnɉ Soo-koomɉ-wit.
What floor is it on?	Yoo chan naiɉ?
It's on the third floor.	Yoo chan sam̄ɉ.
near	glai
far	glai
Is it far?	Glai mai?

Yes./It's far.	Glai.
No./It's not far.	Mai glai.
Go in this side street.	Kao soi nee leuy.
Go a little further.	Pai eeg noi.
Stop/Park here.	Jawt thee-nee.
Could you drive slowly?	Kap cha-cha noi, dai mai?
There's a traffic jam.	Rot tit.

across from	trong kam
around here	thaeoj nee
before a place	gawn theungj
behind	kang langj
between...and..	ra-wang...gap..
downstairs/beneath	kang lang
in front of/facing	kang na
in/inside	nai/kang nai
near to	glai, glai-glai
next to	kang-kang, tit (gap)
outside	kang nawk
past/beyond a place	leuy
upstairs/on top of	kang bon
The bank is next to the hotel.	Tha-na-kan yoo kang-kang rong-raem.
The restaurant is before the intersection.	Ran-a-hanj yoo gawn theungj see-yaek.
The movie theater is in the shopping center.	Rong-nangj yoo kang nai soonj gan ka.

Travel

train	rot-fai
train station	sa-thaɹ-nee rot-fai
first class	chan neung
second class	chan sawngɹ
third class	chan samɹ
sleeping compartment	too nawn
ticket	tuaɹ
classifier for tickets	bai
one-way	thio dio
round trip	pai glap
What time is the train to Surat Thani?	Rot-fai pai Soo-rat Tha-nee gee mong?
I'd like one ticket to Phetburi.	Kawɹ tuaɹ pai Phet-boo-ree neung bai.
How many tickets?	Gee bai?
Two tickets.	Sawngɹ bai.
airplane	kreuang bin
airport	sa-namɹ bin
You have to be at the airport at 7 AM.	Tawng yoo sa-namɹ bin tawn jet mong chao.
city-to-city buses	
regular	rot tham-ma-da
air-conditioned	rot thua
bus station	kiu rot

Is there a bus to Sukothai?	Mee rot pai Soo-koɲ-thai mai?
What time is the bus to Mae Sot?	Rot pai Mae Sawt awk gee mong?
There's a bus at 8 AM.	Rot awk paet mong chao.
There's a bus every hour.	Mee rot awk thook chua-mong.
classifier for vehicles	kun
Which bus? (or any vehicle)	Kun naiɲ?
This bus/vehicle.	Kun nee.
boat	reua
pier	tha reua
Is there a boat to Ko Tao?	Mee reua pai Gaw Tao mai?
classifier for boats	lum
That boat goes to Ko Tao.	Lum nan pai Gaw Tao.
city bus	rot-may
air-conditioned bus	rot-ae
bus route	saiɲ
Which bus goes to the airport?	Saiɲ naiɲ pai sa-namɲ bin?
bus stop ("sign")	pai rot-may

Where's the bus stop? (m)	Pai rot-may yoo thee-naij, krup?
taxi	thaek-see
How much is it to Silom?	Pai Seej-lom thao-rai?
bicycle	jak-gra-yan
motorcycle	maw-teuh-sai
motorcycle helmet	muak gan nawk
car	rot-yon
pick-up with benches	sawngj-thaeoj
Do you have motorcycles for rent?	Mee maw-teuh-sai hai chao mai?
How much is it for one day?	Wan la thao-rai?
arrive at a place	pai theungj
What time will we arrive?	Pai theungj gee mong?
You'll arrive at 6 pm.	Pai theungj tawn hok mong yen.
How long does it take to get to Pattaya?	Pai Phat-tha-ya chai way-la thao-rai?
It takes about two hours.	Chai way-la pra-man sawngj chua-mong.
how far? (how many kilometers?)	gee gee-lo
How far is it to Chiang Saen?	Pai Chiang Saenj gee gee-lo?

It's about fifty kilometers.	Prá-man hǎ-sìp gee-lo.
How much further is it?	Pai eeg gee gee-lo?
Twenty more kilometers.	Eeg yêe-sìp gee-lo.

In Thailand

Bangkok	Groong-thayp
central Thailand	phak glang
northern Thailand	phak neuaɹ
southern Thailand	phak tai, pak tai
northeastern Thailand	phak Ee-sanɹ
eastern Thailand	phak ta-wan awk
province	jang-wat
district	am-pheuh
sub-district	tam-bon
village	moo ban
border	chai-daen
What province are you from?	Koon ma jak jang-wat a-rai?
I'm from Nong Khai province (f).	Chan ma jak jang-wat Nawngɹ Kai.

Hotel

hotel	rong-raem
room	hawng
Do you have a room? (m)	Mee hawng mai, krup?
How much is a room? (f)	Hawng thao-rai, ka?

187

regular room (with fan)	hawng̱ tham-ma-da, hawng̱ phat-lom
air-conditioned room	hawng̱ ae
I'd like an air-conditioned room. (f)	Ao hawng̱ ae, <u>ka</u>.
single bed ("paired beds")	tiang koo
double bed ("one bed")	tiang dio
I'd like a double bed.	Ao tiang dio.
How many nights are you staying?	<u>Yoo</u> gee keun?
I'm staying two nights.	<u>Yoo</u> sawngɟ keun.
towel	pha chet tua
May I have a towel?	<u>Kaw</u>ɟ pha chet tua duay.
key	goon-jae
May I have the key?	<u>Kaw</u>ɟ goon-jae duay.
What's your room number?	Hawng̱ beuh a-rai?
2-0-3	sawngɟ soonɟ samɟ

Home

house	ban
classifier for buildings	langɟ
I live in this house. (f)	Chan <u>yoo</u> ban langɟ nee.
apartment	a-phat-men
room	hawng̱

bathroom	hawng nam
bedroom	hawng nawn
garage	rong rot
kitchen	hawng krua
living room	hawng rap kaek
furniture	feuh-nee-jeuh
bed	tiang
bedsheet	pha poo thee-nawn
blanket	pha hom
broom	mai gwat
bucket	thang
cabinet	too
chair	gao-ee
curtains	pha man
cushion	baw
door	pra-too
floor	pheun
hanger	mai kwaen seua
iron	tao reet
lamp	kom fai
light bulb	lawt fai
mat	seua
mattress	thee-nawn
mirror	gra-jok
pillow	mawn
pillowcase	plawk mawn
pot	maw
refrigerator	too yen

roof	láng-ka
shower fixture	fuk bua
stairs	bun-dai
stove/oven	tao op
table	to
wall (inside)	faj
wall (garden)	gam-phaeng
washing machine	kreuang sak pha
wastebasket	thang ka-ya
water jar	toom
window screen	moong luat
window	na-tang

for rent	hai chao
landlord/landlady	jao kawng ban
I want to rent a house. (f)	Chan yak ja chao ban.
How much is the rent per month?	Ka chao deuan la thao-rai?

Animals

animal	sat
wild animal	sat pa
pet/pets	sat liang
female (animal)	tua mia
male (animal)	tua phoo

ant	mot
bat	kang-kao

bear	mee₁
bee	pheung
bird	nok
butterfly	phee₁ seua
cat	maeo
kitten	look maeo
cockroach	maeng sap
crocodile	jaw-ra-kay
deer	gwang
dog	ma₁, soo-nak
puppy	look ma₁
elephant	chang
fly	ma-laeng wan
frog	gop
goat	phae
horse	ma
insect	ma-laeng
kangaroo	jing-jo
lizard (chameleon)	ging-ga
lizard (large house)	took-gae
lizard (small house)	jing-jok
monkey	ling
mosquito	yoong
mouse/rat	noo₁
owl	nok hook
rabbit	gra-tai
scorpion	maeng pawng
shark	pla cha-lam₁
sheep	gae

snake	ngoo
tiger	seuaj
turtle	tao
whale	pla wan
classifier for animals	tua
How many dogs do you have?	Koon mee maj gee tua?
I have three.	Mee samj tua.

Games & Sports

badminton	baet
ball-kicking game	ta-graw
basketball	bat, bas-get-bawn
boat racing	kaeng reua
to box	chok muay
Thai boxing	muay Thai
international boxing	muay saj-gon
bull fighting (Thai)	chon wua
play cards	len phaj
checkers	mak hawt
chess	mak rook
chicken fighting	chon gai
fighting fish	pla gat
football/soccer	foot-bawn
gamble	len gan pha-nan
golf	gawp
golf course	sa-namj gawp
kite fighting	kaeng wao

sports	gee-la
sports field	sà-nǎmɟ gee-la
swimming	wâi-nam
tennis	then-nít
tennis court	sà-nǎmɟ then-nít
team	theem
referee	gàm-má-gan
What sports do you like?	Koon châwp gee-la a-rai?
I like soccer.	Châwp foot-bawn.
beat/win	chá-ná
lose (to)	phae
Who won?	Krai chá-ná?
Our team won.	Theem kawngɟ rao chá-ná.
The Malaysian team lost.	Theem Ma-lay-sia phae.

Weather

weather	a-gàt
The weather's good today.	Wan-nee a-gàt dee
It's hot.	A-gàt rawn.
It's cool.	A-gàt yen.
It's cold.	A-gàt naoɟ.
degree (temperature)	ong-saɟ
What's the temperature?	Oon-hà-phoom thâo-rái?
It's 30 degrees.	Sǎmɟ-sìp ong-saɟ.

rain	fonɉ
It's raining.	Fonɉ tòk.
It's raining hard.	Fonɉ tòk nák.
It stopped raining.	Fonɉ yòot laeo.
It's going to rain.	Fonɉ jà tòk.
Last night it rained.	Meuá-keun-nee fonɉ tòk.
Do you think it's going to rain?	Koon kit wā fonɉ jà tòk mai?
No, I don't think it's going to rain.	Kit wā mai tòk.
wind (n)	lom
There's some wind.	Lom phát.
The wind is blowing hard.	Lom raeng.
storm	pha-yoo
A storm is coming.	Pha-yoo jà ma.
sunshine	daet
It's sunny.	Daet awk.
There's no sun.	Daet mai awk.
clouds	mayk
It's cloudy.	Mee mayk mak.
flood	nam thuam
dew	nam kang
fog	mawk
snow	hee-ma
lightning	fa laep
thunder	fa rawng
rainbow	roong

THAI PHRASEBOOK

season	nȃ, reu-doo
hot season	nȃ rawn
rainy season	nȃ fŏnɉ
cold season	nȃ naoɉ
What season is this?	Nȃ nee nȃ a-rai?
This is the hot season.	Nȃ nee nȃ fŏnɉ.

Thai Culture

temple fair	ngan wȃt
make merit (in Buddhism)	tham boon
give food to monks	tham boon tȁk bȁt
ordination party	ngan bȕat nȁk
amulet	phra kreuang
flower garland	phuang ma-lai
spirit house	sanɉ-phra-phoom
city pillar	lȁk meuang
string tying ceremony	bai-seeɉ soo kwanɉ
tying strings on wrists	phook kaw meu
Central Thai opera	lee-gay
Southern Thai opera	ma-no-ra
Chinese opera	ngiuɉ
masked dancing	konɉ
shadow puppet play	nangɉ ta-loong
traditional circle dance	ram-wong
Naga (serpent)	nȁk
giant/ogre	yȁk
Hanuman (monkey god)	Ha-noo-man
singha (lion)	singɉ

195

Thai country music	look thoong
Lao/Eesan music	mawj lum
Thai orchestra	wong pee-phat
cymbals	ching, chap
xylophone	ra-nat
bamboo mouth organ	kaen
Thai New Year	Songj-gran
throw water	rot nam
Krathong holiday	loi gra-thong

Religion

religion	sat-sa-naj
Buddhism	sat-sa-naj Phoot
Christianity	sat-sa-naj Krit
Islam	sat-sa-naj It-sa-lam
Judaism	sat-sa-naj Yiu
What's your religion?	Koon nap-theuj sat-sa-naj a-rai?
I'm a Buddhist. (f)	Chan nap-theuj sat-sa-naj Phoot.
temple compound	wat
temple building	bot ("boat")
monk's quarters	goo-tee
monk	phra
nun	mae chee
novice	nayn, samj-ma-nayn
be ordained	buat
meditate	nang sa-ma-thee

chant	suat mon
morning alms round	bin tha bat
dharma	tham-ma
karma	gam
pagoda/stupa	je-dee
the Buddha	Phra Phoot-tha-jao
statue of the Buddha	Phra Phoot-tha-roop
reclining Buddha	Phra nawn
Pali (language)	Ba-lee
Sanskrit (language)	Sunj-sa-grit
Muslim	Moot-sa-lim
mosque	soo-rao, mas-yeet
Koran	An Goo-ra-an
Allah	Phra Al-law
Mohammed	Mo-ha-mut
Christian	kon nap-theuj
	sat-sa-naj Krit
church	bot
go to church	kao bot
Jesus	Phra Yay-soo
Bible	Phra Kam-phee
Christmas	Krit-sa-mat

Hippocrene Children's Illustrated Japanese
Dictionary
English-Japanese/Japanese-English
96 pages • 8½ x 11 • ISBN 0-7818-0817-0 • $14.95hc • (31)

Japanese-English/English-Japanese Concise
Dictionary, Romanized
**8,000 entries • 235 pages • 4 x 6 • ISBN 0-7818-0162-1 •
$11.95pb • (474)**

Beginner's Japanese
290 pages • 6 x 8 • ISBN 0-7818-0234-2 • $11.95pb • (53)

Mastering Japanese
339 pages • 5½ x 8½ • ISBN 0-87052-923-4 • $14.95pb • (523)
2 cassettes: **ISBN 0-87052-983-8 • $12.95 • (524)**

Japanese Handy Dictionary
**3,400 entries • 120 pages • 5 x 7 • ISBN 0-87052-962-5 •
$8.95pb • (466)**

Korean-English/English-Korean Practical
Dictionary
**8,500 entries • 365 pages • 4 x 7¼ • ISBN 0-87052-092-X •
$14.95pb • (399)**

Korean-English/English-Korean Handy Dictionary
**4,000 entries • 178 pages • 5 x 8 • ISBN 0-7818-0082-X •
$8.95pb • (438)**

Lao-English/English-Lao Dictionary and
Phrasebook
**2,500 entries • 207 pages • 3¾ x 7 • ISBN 0-7818-0858-8 •
$12.95pb • (179)**

Lao Basic Course
350 pages • 5 x 8 • ISBN 0-7818-0410-8 • $19.95pb • (470)

Malay-English/English-Malay Standard Dictionary
**21,000 entries • 631 pages • 5 x 7¼ • ISBN 0-7818-0103-6 •
$16.95pb • (428)**

Pilipino-English/English-Pilipino Concise
Dictionary
**5,000 entries • 389 pages • 4 x 6 • ISBN 0-87052-491-7 •
$8.95pb • (393)**

Pilipino-English/English-Pilipino Dictionary and Phrasebook
2,200 entries • 186 pages • 3¾ x 7 • ISBN 0-7818-0451-5 • $11.95pb • (295)

Concise Sanskrit-English Dictionary
18,000 entries • 366 pages • 5 x 7 • ISBN 0-7818-0203-2 • $14.95pb • (605)

Tagalog-English/English-Tagalog (Pilipino) Standard Dictionary
20,000 entries • 363 pages • 5½ x 8½ • ISBN 0-7818-0657-7 • $14.95pb • (5)

Beginner's Vietnamese
517 pages • 7 x 10 • ISBN 0-7818-0411-6 • $19.95pb • (253)

Vietnamese-English/English-Vietnamese Standard Dictionary
12,000 entries • 501 pages • 5 x 7 • ISBN 0-87052-924-2 • $19.95pb • (529)

All prices subject to change without prior notice. To purchase **Hippocrene Books** contact your local bookstore, call (718) 454-2366, visit www.hippocrenebooks.com, or write to: Hippocrene Books, 171 Madison Avenue, New York, NY 10016. Please enclose check or money order, adding $5.00 shipping (UPS) for the first book and $.50 for each additional book.